D0538441

NOT ON LOVE ALONE

∞

NOT ON LOVE ALONE

A COOKBOOK

A Year of Delicious Dinners and More for Newlyweds

Jessie Carry Saunders

MARLOWE & COMPANY
NEW YORK

NOT ON LOVE ALONE: *A Year of Delicious Dinners and More for Newlyweds*
Copyright © 2005 by Jessie Carry Saunders

Published by
Marlowe & Company
An Imprint of Avalon Publishing Group Incorporated
245 West 17th Street • 11th Floor
New York, NY 10011-5300

AVALON
publishing group incorporated

Library of Congress Cataloging-in-Publication Data
Saunders, Jessie Carry, 1976-
  Not on love alone : a cookbook : a year of delicious dinners and more for newlyweds /
Jessie Carry Saunders.
    p. cm.
  Includes bibliographical references and index.
  ISBN 1-56924-375-1 (hardcover : alk. paper)
  1. Cookery for two. I. Title.

TX652.S287 2005
641.'612—dc22

2005000279

9 8 7 6 5 4 3 2 1

Designed by Pauline Neuwirth, Neuwirth and Associates, Inc.

Printed in Italy

Contents

INTRODUCTION   1

    Must-Have Kitchen Items   6

    Master Pantry   8

    A Note on Dinner Parties   12

JANUARY: *Comfort Food, High and Low*   13

FEBRUARY: *The Atkins Counterrevolution*   27

MARCH: *A Fish Tale*   45

APRIL: *Early Birds*   61

MAY: *Déjeuner sur l'Herbe*   81

    Summer Pantry   96

JUNE: *Midsummer and Midnight*   97

JULY: *Vacation, All I Ever Wanted*   115

AUGUST: *On Our Best (or Worst) Behavior*   132

SEPTEMBER: *Italian-Indian Summer*   155

OCTOBER: *Rabbit Stew vs. Rabbit Food*   169

NOVEMBER: *Home for the Holidays*   187

    Winter Pantry   200

DECEMBER: *The Big Payback*   203

ANNIVERSARY: *And Many More*   228

To JS, who is always a pleasure to feed

Acknowledgments

MANY, MANY THANKS TO: Johnny, Mom, Pops, Will, Patty Madsen, Debbie Brown, Pat Stewart, Mary Ellen Van Buskirk, Callie Haines, Isabelle and Ronny Krishana, Weatherly Ralph, Joyce Chang, Simone Vairon, Mag Rochereau, Francoise Payen, Betsy Newell; my editor, Kylie Foxx, my publisher, Matthew Lore, and everyone at Avalon; Pauline Neuwirth of Neuwirth Associates, for the spot-on book design; and Susi Oberhelman, for designing the beautiful cover. And I wouldn't be eating so well or so often without my friends on Bleecker Street at Murray's Cheese Shop and Ottomanelli's Meat Market.

NOT ON LOVE ALONE

∞

Introduction

THIS IS A cookbook for newly married people. It's not a cookbook for newly married people in the way that the *Joy of Cooking* is—that is, it's not an encyclopedic listing of all the food you might ever make in your entire lives. Instead, it's a book about *meals*—about eating together, about feeding your friends, and about having a life at the dinner table, all year round.

A take-out existence is a monotonous one. It makes you sluggish and, if you believe your mother, will give you bad skin. *But,* some argue, *it's easy. We don't have time. We're busy.* Balderdash.

Cooking for yourselves, and sitting down and eating it with each other, is what this book is all about. It doesn't have to be an investment of hours—some of the best meals are prepared in minutes. But sitting down with your honey keeps you happy. It means you talk to each other face to face, and not just on your cell phones. You get to flirt. And eat. Food is love, after all.

And don't I know it.

When my husband, JS, and I first met in college, he pointed out a peculiarity of mine to me. "Whenever you talk about your vacations," he said, "the only thing you ever mention is the food you ate while you were there."

I protested, but he was prepared. He had proof. He reminded me of a trip

I'd taken recently with my parents, to a chalet in the Italian Alps. Some people might have been impressed by the majesty of the mountains, the breathtaking green of the valleys, et cetera, but the only thing I remembered was this small dish of fresh pasta with squash blossoms and butter I'd eaten as part of my dinner. I'd gone on and on about it. What was in it? Could I make it at home? Had I mentioned how good it was?

I blame this food fanaticism on my father. I started in the kitchen at my father's knee. Probably literally—I was a very short kid. Growing up, Pops was the cook in the family, working the huge Garland range in our apartment like a mad wizard. Emphasis on *mad*. My father's explosions at the stove were legendary in our family, making every stereotype out there about Irish temperaments ring true. Adding my mother to the mix was a Bad Idea. Her tentative overtures to help were loudly rebuffed. Somehow, however, I snuck in. Perhaps it was because I was so short. I was soon put to work. One of my first duties was making salad dressing: pouring all the ingredients into a jar, screwing the lid on tightly, and shaking as hard as I could for what seemed like hours. Since those days, Pops and I have cooked very happily together. He gets mad, I calm him down, and everybody eats.

As Pops worked rather late when we were little, my brother Will and I ate his cooking only on special occasions and, in the summer, on vacation. Normally, Will and I ate together earlier in the evening, dining on whatever Mom made for us. Will's little trick was swallowing his peas whole so he didn't have to taste them.

But later in the evening, when Pops got home, he and Mom would eat together—in the dining room!—complete with mood lighting and place mats. Watching two adults eat like this throughout my early childhood made a big impression on me: This is what adults do!

I introduced JS to this habit early on. One summer, he was working in Knoxville, Tennessee, and I flew out to visit him with a hunk of Parmesan, a sack of Arborio rice, and a bottle of good red wine from my parents in my luggage. We sat at his rented kitchen table and ate homemade risotto and drank good wine and everything was right with the world.

So I believe in eating together. JS believes in eating whatever I cook, period, which is a compatible philosophy. I understand it can seem difficult to get it together enough to make a meal and sit down—work, social obligations, important baseball playoff games all intrude—but even a simple menu of soup and salad eaten away from the television will mean twenty minutes of behaving like a couple rather than like roommates.

Of course eating together is not the same as cooking together. Some people are endlessly entertained by chopping carrots, peeling apples, or kneading dough. Some people think those people are absolutely crazy. Sometimes these people are married to each other.

Cooking together, working side by side in harmonious silence, in a cheerful, warm kitchen, is a wonderful fantasy that might play out in some households. But in my experience (father, Irish temper, et cetera) cooks can be cranky when other people stick their oar in. The stove is the cook's stronghold, hostile to invaders, no matter how well-meaning. Cooks like things their way. They want to flip the pancakes, cook the bacon perfectly, squeeze the juice just so.

But as long as they're making that meal for you, why complain? This, I'm sure, is the attitude of JS, the man who asks for guidance when heating a can of Campbell's. In fact, the most important role the non-cook can play is that of cooking enabler—doing everything he or she can to make sure the cook will cook again. Even if the idea of sautéing or steaming gives JS hives, rinsing off some dishes or washing a pot after dinner is the least he can do after the nice dinner he's just devoured. And he looks cute in an apron.

Sometimes JS comes grocery shopping with me. We live right off of Bleeker Street in New York City. Right near us are some of the best butchers, fishmongers, and cheese shops in the country, and as I pop into one and then the other, JS dutifully carries his future dinner around the neighborhood. Then he dutifully carries it up five flights of stairs.

Eating together should never mean all pleasure for one, all drudgery for the other. And, in the brave new age of TiVo, dinner need never be rushed in favor of the game or a rerun of *The Simpsons*. Linger a little.

Enjoy each other. Have a civilized conversation about more than the dry cleaning or the cable repairman. It's a recipe for a happy marriage.

To start you on the way to eternal wedded bliss, foodwise, I've come up with menus and dishes for each month of the first year of marriage. Sometimes I've provided the whole shebang—starter, main course, dessert—but other times I've just suggested things and left the details to your own interpretation. Do you feel like a salad? What about some cheese? How involved you make the meal can be up to you.

Some of the menus are more complicated than others, but they all have one thing in common—they're not fussy. Eating at home is about eating elegantly, but not laboriously. I leave the pyrotechnics to the real chefs in the restaurants—and for sanity's sake, so should you.

Besides, a big part of becoming comfortable in the kitchen is learning what flavors you like, and how to combine them without necessarily relying on your tablespoons or (God forbid) cookbooks. It's about what things smell like, look like, feel like in your mouth when you're tasting them. I hope this book will lead you to that kind of confidence.

My Kitchen

Nobody works under ideal circumstances. As proof, I offer up my stove. It came with my apartment, and I kept it because it fits so well. This is also a kitchen with an eighteen-inch dishwasher, a mini-microwave, and a refrigerator that's only twenty-two inches wide. You can see, in the accompanying drawing (not to scale), its impressive dimensions.

20"

22"

40 ½"

NO THERMOSTAT

PUT HAND ·and· LIT MATCH IN HERE

Like all stoves, it has some quirks. Its main idiosyncrasy is its lack of a thermostat in the oven, with the added attraction of having no pilot light. I've developed an elaborate process of sticking my hand—holding a lit match—into the belly of the oven to light it; then, after escaping injury, achieving a constant temperature by fiddling with the knob, propping the oven door open with a wooden spoon, and, every once in a while, with the aid of a flashlight, checking the hanging thermometer I've installed on the single rack.

Also, it's on a slight angle. Whether that's the fault of the building or of the oven, I'm not sure. Both have been here for many decades. Every cake comes out just a bit lopsided. That doesn't stop me from baking them, though.

⌐ MUST-HAVE KITCHEN ITEMS ⌐

HERE ARE SOME things I can't live without in the kitchen. My advice is that you return that panini maker you registered for and get these instead:

UTENSILS

Food mill: Applesauce. Tomato sauce. Any puree that wants just the best parts of the food with the undesirables—seeds, pits, and skin—left behind.

Stainless-steel pepper grinder: For all your fresh peppercorns. It'll last forever and looks great, too.

Bamboo-handled strainer: A cheap investment that comes in handy almost daily

Good heatproof rubber spatulas: For scraping down the sides of hot pans or cold bowls

Mandoline: In its less-expensive incarnation (available at cookware stores like Williams-Sonoma) a mando-line is essentially a slab of plastic with a cutting blade imbedded in it. It's the easiest way to slice potatoes, apples, fennel, celery root, or any other hard fruit or vegetable paper thin.

Good pair of tongs: Almost an appendage to your arm, you can use them to turn chicken cutlets or toss salad greens.

SPRING HINGE HERE

Good chef's knife: Cutting ingredients with a dull blade is not only frustrating, it's dangerous.

Vegetable peeler: Surprisingly versatile. Think of it for curls of chocolate or Parmesan cheese as well as peeling carrots.

Kitchen shears: Not just for opening packages any more. Snip parsley, cut up canned tomatoes, matchstick bacon, the uses go on and on.

Instant-read meat thermometer: The only way you'll really know your chicken is done.

POTS, PANS, ET CETERA

My father gave me a deluxe set of All-Clad cookware, one of my favorite presents of all time. If you're wise, you registered for something similar, with heavy bottoms so you don't have the pleasure of scraping burnt food off the pots with Brillo every evening.

In general, you should have:

Large frying pan or skillet (with a lid)
Small frying pan
Nonstick frying pan
Medium-size saucepan (with a lid)
Large pot (at least 6 quarts) with a lid for braising,
    stocks, and boiling water for pasta

Want more? Try:

Cast-iron frying pan
Enameled cast-iron casserole, like those from Le Creuset
Grill pan or griddle that will give you authentic-looking grill lines
Pot specifically for pasta, with a large colander insert for draining

Master Pantry

YOU DON'T NEED me to tell you about all the basic things you should have on hand on a regular basis. I assume you can handle the purchase of your baking powder or granulated sugar. Instead, I've listed and described twenty foods—some quite simple—that I use again and again, and with which you would do well to stock your pantry.

Arborio Rice: The wide world of rice extends beyond the boil-in-a-bag variety. Arborio rice is a very starchy, short-grained rice from Italy, used in one of my favorite dishes: risotto.

Basmati Rice: You can buy this in big bins at the supermarket and use it as your basic, everyday rice. There's no competition between this and converted rice in terms of taste and smell.

Pasta: The ultimate cheap and filling dinner, I like to spend an extra buck or two and get artisanal pastas—which are available more and more everywhere—because of their superior taste and texture. Get a whole bunch of different shapes for different sauces.

Nuts: Particularly pine nuts, whole almonds, hazelnuts, and pecans. All raw and unsalted, they keep best in the freezer, where they'll remain fresh (the oils in nuts go rancid very quickly).

Lemons: My refrigerator is a forest of half-used lemons. A squeeze of lemon brightens up the dreariest of dishes, and lemons make your kitchen smell wonderful.

Fresh Ginger: Well-wrapped in your fridge, ginger adds a punch of freshness to meals. I like a bit of it grated over sugared pears for dessert.

Shallots: The smaller, violet-colored friend of the onion, their sweetness is perfect for sautéing and for salad dressings.

Onions: I like to have both red and yellow onions on hand. Keep them in a cool, dry place.

Garlic: I usually buy my garlic at the Union Square Greenmarket, where I know the garlic is top quality. When you buy it at your local greengrocer, make sure the head is firm and that there are no obvious shoots poking out of the papery skin—shoots mean the garlic has germinated and has lost some of its oomph.

Greek Yogurt: This is thicker and richer than normal yogurt (even when it's fat-free) and comes in handy as a base for salad dressings, marinades, and sauces. Not surprisingly, it's also nice for breakfast topped with berries and honey.

Unsalted Butter: I use unsalted, or sweet, butter—your basic Land o' Lakes—for baking and general cooking, and occasionally a snooty fancy French butter, higher in milk fat, for impressing people or winning over new friends.

Sea Salt: I talk more about this later, but for salads and finishing off dishes, a sprinkle of real sea salt is the best. Just walk right past the package with the umbrella-toting girl and look for something better.

Kosher Salt: This is my basic cooking salt. It dissolves instantaneously and has a gentle salinity that makes oversalting difficult to do.

Canned Tomatoes: Highest-quality plum tomatoes, canned in Italy, are the cook's salvation ten months of the year. You could use mealy pink hothouse tomatoes in that recipe . . . or a can of perfect plums! The choice is up to you.

 Sherry Vinegar: There's a smoky fruitiness to this vinegar that makes it my favorite. I always go for it, leaving the bottles of white and red wine vinegars on my shelf terribly neglected.

Olive Oil: These days, everyone has an olive oil fetish, with fancy gold-wrapped bottles going for more than the price of a decent meal. I avoid the nutsiness, though I do buy a more elegant, fruity olive oil for lettuce salads.

Hazelnut Oil: This sounds obscure, but it's my favorite alternate salad oil—slightly amber, delicate, and just a bit sweet. Use it when you don't want olive oil to be the dominant flavor.

Peppercorns: Sometimes I use black peppercorns, sometimes I'm beguiled by the multicolored variety. Either way, they should be fresh and ground in a good pepper grinder, or used whole. No precracked or ground pepper, please. Such things make me very sad.

Fresh Thyme: You can now get this by the bale-full year-round in every corner of the country, it seems, and so much the better. The fresh has a softer flavor, although the dried is perfectly respectable in a pinch.

Herbes de Provence: There's something about the balance of all those summer flavors dried and condensed into one little jar that is very pleasing when added in small doses to chicken or lamb.

⌁ A NOTE ON DINNER PARTIES ⌁

JS AND I are dinner-party givers. We pack 'em into our tiny kitchen, where, once seated, everyone has a job to do—the wine de-corker, for instance, or the bread cutter—since too many people standing at once is a recipe for disaster. If I want eight for dinner, JS needs to disassemble my desk to add to the end of our kitchen table, and we have been known to enlist our bedside tables (formerly Chinese garden stools) as seating. As long as you strategically place any left-handers, a good time will be had by all.

A dinner party is a very personal thing—it's an expression of your own tastes and preferences. But here are a few general tips that have served me well:

- *Be available*. Try to cook ahead as much as humanly possible, and reheat as necessary. The several recipes I give here for braised meats and stews are perfect for dinner parties, as they're often better after a little sitting. Your friends want to see *you*, not see you sweating over a stove. If people ask to help, give them a quick task that takes a few minutes—lighting candles, slicing bread, that sort of thing. They help, but they're also drinking and socializing at the same time. Any last-minute concentration should be performed by you.

- *Be leisurely.* Don't rush people to the table and, once there, don't rush through dinner. No galloping gourmet here.

- *Be moderate.* Particularly when you're feeding people several courses, don't weigh down their plates with food. Serve reasonable portions and offer seconds. People feel guilty if they don't eat everything on their plates, and if you give them half a chicken, chances are they won't be able to finish it.

NOT ON LOVE ALONE

January

Comfort Food, High and Low

Comfort Food, High and Low

THE MOST CLICHÉD comfort food in the American imagination is meat loaf. I think of it in all those 1950s commercials, surrounded by instant mashed potatoes and canned peas. It always looks very gray.

But of course, my favorite comfort food is meat loaf, and when I asked JS, he said meat loaf right away, too (though I tried to convince him it was the shredded wheat with hot milk and butter his father used to make him). Simply put, we're meat loaf people, and we eat it with mashed potatoes and peas (though I do have my pride—I make the mashed potatoes from scratch).

Still, it's one thing to make meat loaf (or any other lowly comfort food) for yourselves on a Sunday night, and quite another to whip up a meat loaf and serve it to your friends on Friday. So while there's a place for the low, there's also a place for the high. In the first menu, I've rejiggered comfort food so that your guests leave full, warm, and happy, but also impressed by your deft handling of shiitake mushrooms. Then, I gave recipes for two foods, chicken noodle soup and applesauce, which are quintessential everyday comfort foods. They are so much better made at home than anywhere else, it would be a shame not to have them in your repertoire. They'll always cheer you up if you're sick or grumpy. (And if you want a perfect meat loaf recipe, you don't need me for that—it already exists in *The Fannie Farmer Cookbook*. Give it a try.)

Haute Homestyle

WATERCRESS SALAD WITH SMOKED TROUT (PAGE 16)
❧
BRAISED VEAL WITH MUSHROOM RAGOUT AND GARLIC TOASTS (PAGE 18)
❧
LACE COOKIES (PAGE 21)

Essential Comforts

CHICKEN NOODLE SOUP, OR CURE FOR THE COMMON COLD (PAGE 22)
❧
APPLESAUCE (PAGE 26)

HAUTE HOMESTYLE

~

Watercress Salad with Smoked Trout

The smoked fish is the comfort food in this salad. It might just be the New Yorker in me, but I love all sorts of smoked fish, and we always had it at home, particularly the smoked trout and Nova salmon from Murray's Sturgeon Shop on Broadway. The textures and the flavors here are bright but not intimidating. It's the perfect dinner party dish.

FOR THE SAUCE:

½ cup sour cream

1 tablespoon horseradish

1 tablespoon chopped fresh dill

A squeeze of fresh lemon juice

A small pinch of salt

FOR THE SALAD:

1 whole smoked trout, filleted (making 2 fillets)

1 Granny Smith apple

3 cups watercress leaves (no stems), well picked over, washed, and dried

1 tablespoon hazelnut oil (you can substitute a light olive oil)

A squeeze of fresh lemon juice (about 2 teaspoons), plus extra for the apple

Salt and pepper to taste

1. Make the sauce for the trout: In a small bowl, combine all the ingredients, being shy with the salt—the trout itself is quite salty. Taste the sauce—it should have some zing, and you can augment the horseradish and lemon as you like. Refrigerate it until you need it.
2. Break up the trout fillets. Leave some meaty-looking pieces—you don't want to shred it or make it look like tuna salad. Set aside.
3. Slice the apple: On a cutting board with the apple standing stem up, make 4 cuts straight down in a box around the core; toss the core. You'll have 2 large and 2 smaller pieces of apple. Placing them cut side down on the cutting board, slice

thin crescents of apple (you might ditch the tiniest ones). Sprinkle the slices with a bit of lemon juice to keep them from turning unpleasantly brown.

4. In a salad bowl, toss the watercress with the hazelnut oil and the lemon juice, adding just a grind of pepper and a few grains of salt. The salad should be very lightly dressed.

5. Now assemble the salad on plates: A small handful of watercress should go on the plate first, followed by 4 or 5 slices of apple placed so they lean against the mound of salad (be as fussy about this as you like). Then, put a small pool of the horseradish sauce at the base of the apples and pile a serving of the smoked trout on top.

TIME: *Leave yourself 15 minutes to commune with the watercress; otherwise, this goes very fast and is almost entirely make-ahead.*
FEEDS: *4 as a first course*

Braised Veal with Mushroom Ragout and Garlic Toasts

Sometimes, rice doesn't seem quite right . . . nor does pasta . . . and you can't be bothered to peel potatoes. That's when I fall back on my favorite starchy accompaniment: bread. In this case, I gussy it up by toasting it and rubbing it with garlic. The veal itself is very easy to make, as long as you're careful and keep the heat low so the meat cooks very gently and slowly.

3 tablespoons olive oil

5 tablespoons butter

3-lb. piece of veal shoulder, tied by the butcher (you might want to order this in advance)

3 strips of lemon peel (no pith!)

Several sprigs fresh thyme

5 cloves garlic, peeled: 3 crushed, 1 whole, and 1 chopped

⅔ cup dry white wine

5 cups assorted mushrooms (I suggest a mix of cremini, white, shiitake, and oyster, but a full complement of white is perfectly delicious), cut into half-dollar size

6 slices of country bread, ½ inch thick (if the bread is very large, use ½ slice per serving)

4 shallots, chopped

Handful chopped fresh flat-leaf parsley

Salt and pepper, to taste

1. Put 2 tablespoons of the olive oil, plus 1 tablespoon butter, in the bottom of a casserole and place over medium-high heat. Once the fat is hot, salt and pepper the veal roast, and place it in the casserole; brown it on all sides, about 15 minutes total. (A combination of tongs and a two-pronged fork is a capable way to wrestle with turning the meat.) Turn down the heat slightly if the butter solids get too brown.

2. Remove the roast to a plate and add the lemon peel, thyme, and the 3 crushed garlic cloves to the pot, turning a few times in the fat until you smell the lemon and garlic. Put the veal back in the pot, and add the white wine. Bring to a boil and put the cover on, turning down the heat to a minimum. Let it cook—if you peek into the pot, you should see 4 or 5 small streams of bubbles gently rising to the top.

3. If you're bored—as there will be nothing to do for several hours—you can prep the mushrooms by wiping them off and cutting them into large pieces. If you're using shiitakes, remove the stems and discard; otherwise just trim the stems so they look

Not on Love Alone

presentable. You can also prepare the garlic toasts. If you have a grill pan, that's excellent—you can grill the bread on it and make lovely decorative grill marks. Or you can toast it in the toaster oven. Halve the whole garlic clove and, while the toasts are still warm, rub them with the garlic. Set aside at room temperature.

4. Let the veal cook, turning it occasionally, for 2 hours. Around the 1½-hour mark, turn the heat up slightly (to low, instead of very low) and leave the lid ajar. At the end of 2 hours, the veal should be very tender and cooked through. It should give gracefully under pressure from the back of your fork or stirring spoon.

5. Remove the veal from the pot and place it on a platter (this is just temporary). Pour the cooking juices off into a bowl and reserve (taste for salt content, and add seasoning as needed). Turn up the heat on the pot to medium high. Add the remaining olive oil, and when it's hot, add the shallot and chopped garlic. Stir for a few moments, and when you can smell the garlic, add the mushrooms. Let everything sizzle for a moment, then add the remaining butter on top of the mushrooms. After 30 seconds, give them a good toss for about 5 minutes. (I find that adding the butter on top of the mushrooms prevents the few on the bottom from absorbing all the fat immediately, and thus distributes it nicely.) Add some salt and pepper, to taste. Add the braising liquid back to the pan (you can discard the sorry-looking lemon peel and garlic cloves at this point). Put the roast back in the pot on top of the mushrooms. Put the lid on the pot, then stick it on the back burner on minimum heat for at least 30 minutes.

6. To serve: fish the veal out of the casserole and, starting from either end, try your best to slice it prettily into ⅓-inch slices, though it might fall apart immediately. Cut a toast in half, laying one half slightly on top of the other. Add a serving of veal, then ladle a generous helping of mushrooms and sauce over the top—enough to soak the toast. Add some parsley for color, repeat with the remaining plates, and you're ready to go.

⁓

SPECIAL EQUIPMENT: *A good enameled cast-iron casserole or heavy-bottomed pot.*
TIME: *Give yourself at least 3 hours to make this dish, mostly unattended. It can be made ahead and gently reheated at serving time.*
FEEDS: *4 very hungry lumberjacks, or 6 civilized dinner-party guests. The leftovers are great shredded into tomato sauce as a luxurious ragout for pasta.*

Beef and Veal Cuts to Braise

〜

Whenever I visit my butcher's, the venerable Ottomanelli's Meat Market on Bleecker Street, Frank, Jerry, and Peter always stand by patiently as I peruse the refrigerated compartments looking for dinner. Normally, I zoom right past the duck breasts and beef tenderloins in favor of something more . . . everyday.

CHUCK ROAST
(BEEF)

This usually means fattier pieces of meat—nothing you would eat rare—that need to sit in a hot bath of braising liquid for several hours in order to become tender. Basically, I mean pot roast. The veal and mushroom recipe is essentially fancier pot roast with a younger cow. Remember what Barbra Streisand says in *Funny Girl* after she eats some French pâté? "It's just chopped liver!"

BONELESS
RUMP ROAST
(BEEF)

So, which cuts? If you're scouring the supermarket meat case, look for beef chuck or rump roasts, in that order, even better if they're still on the bone. You could also go for a brisket. With veal roast, you could try some shoulder, as in the preceding recipe, or a veal breast, which is very succulent on the bone but occasionally harder to find.

VEAL BREAST

BONELESS
SHOULDER
(VEAL)

Lace Cookies

Perfect with ice cream, and wonderfully nutty and chewy.

½ stick unsalted butter, softened

⅔ cup packed light brown sugar

⅓ cup white sugar

1 egg

1 cup finely chopped walnuts and pecans

2 tablespoons all-purpose flour

1 teaspoon vanilla extract

1. Preheat the oven to 350°F. Before you start baking, either prepare two nonstick pans by very lightly greasing them, or line two cookie sheets with parchment paper, then grease the paper amply. Don't be shy about this, because to say that these are sticky cookies is an understatement.
2. In a mixing bowl, cream the butter and sugars with a wooden spoon. Mix in the egg. Then add the chopped nuts, flour, and vanilla extract, and stir until just combined.
3. Drop the batter in 1-teaspoon blobs (a soup spoon is good for this) on your prepared cookie sheets. These puppies should be at least 3 inches from each other or you'll have cookie collisions. Throw them in the oven and bake for 10 to 12 minutes, checking after 8 minutes to see that they're not too dark. A dark nonstick pan will make the cookies bake faster than light-colored parchment. Don't underbake them, or they'll never come off the sheet.
4. Pull the cookies from the oven and let cool for several minutes until you pop them off the parchment, or remove them from the nonstick cookie sheet using a very thin spatula. If you need to use the cookie sheet again for another batch, let it cool a few minutes longer, and regrease it if need be (used butter wrappers are very handy for this) before the next round.

SPECIAL EQUIPMENT: *Nonstick cookie sheets are highly useful here, since these cookies are all sugar, but you can use cookie sheets lined with parchment instead.*

TIME: *Barely any at all! 15 minutes, start to finish.*

FEEDS: *This recipe makes 4 dozen cookies, so it depends what sort of binge you're on. If you don't eat them all at once, they will last in an airtight container for several weeks.*

ESSENTIAL COMFORTS

aving eaten many cans of chicken soup and many, many jars of applesauce in my life, I need eat no more. You don't need to, either. The real deals—the stuff you make yourself on a Sunday afternoon—are so far removed from the pale supermarket imitations that once you taste them, you won't go back. The bonus? They're almost impossible to mess up.

Chicken Noodle Soup, or Cure for the Common Cold

When you have the midwinter sniffles, eating chicken soup is definitely more fun than downing Robitussin or Nyquil, and probably better for you, too. The best part about the following recipe (and the applesauce recipe as well) is that it freezes like a champ and is always ready when you need it.

This is my mother's recipe and she hates celery, so there's no celery in the finished product (she throws it away after the chicken broth is done). But if you're partial to celery, please feel free to add some in at the end. Just know my mother wouldn't approve.

Several sprigs fresh flat-leaf parsley

Several sprigs fresh thyme

Bay leaf

15 peppercorns

5 lbs. chicken parts—wings, backs, necks—including a whole chicken breast on the bone

3 carrots, peeled and cut into 3-inch sections

2 celery stalks

1 large onion, peeled

2 whole cloves, stuck into aforementioned onion

1 clove garlic, in its papery skin

2 cups dried egg noodles

1 tablespoon kosher salt

A bit of chopped fresh flat-leaf parsley, to taste

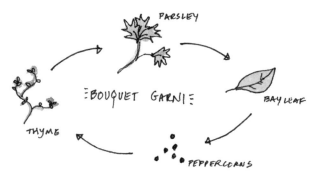

1. Make a bouquet garni: Cut a square of cheesecloth large enough to contain the parsley, thyme, bay leaf, and peppercorns, then cut a longish length of kitchen string and tie the cheesecloth closed like a little hobo bag. Leave a long end of string that you can tie to the handle of your stockpot. Set it aside.

2. Put the chicken in your stockpot along with all the vegetables. Tie the bouquet garni leash to the pot and let the herbs join the fun. Add cold water to the pot until the ingredients are covered by at least 1 inch of water. Fire up the stove.

3. Bring that baby to a boil, then turn it down to the barest simmer. As the pot is coming up to a boil and for about the first 30 minutes, the stock will create a scummy foam. Be diligent and skim it off with a spoon until it ceases.

4. Simmer the stock for 2½ to 3 hours, uncovered. About an hour and a half into the cooking, remove the chicken breasts and keep them covered until you need them. Add more water as necessary to keep the ingredients covered. And keep on skimming—there's no more scum, but plenty of yellow chicken fat rises to the top of the broth. Do this with a soup spoon every 20 minutes or so, particularly if you're planning on eating the soup the same day.

5. Strain the soup through a cheesecloth-lined sieve into a large bowl or another large pot. Save the carrots, but discard everything else from the stockpot.

6. To finish the soup, heat the strained stock to a boil, and add the egg noodles and kosher salt. While the noodles are cooking, slice the carrots into ¼-inch rounds and skin and tear the reserved chicken breast into generous bite-size pieces. As the noodles finish cooking—they'll take only 5 to 7 minutes—turn down the heat to low and add the carrots and chicken. Taste for salt.

7. Ladle the soup into bowls, adding a punch of green with some chopped parsley if you're so inclined.

SPECIAL EQUIPMENT: *Cheesecloth, kitchen string, and a stockpot.*
TIME: *An afternoon, but almost entirely unattended*
FEEDS: *The 2 of you 4 or more times over the course of the month if frozen*

Variations on a Chicken Soup Theme

MAKING YOUR OWN chicken stock sounds like something only pretentious home cooks would do, but it's very easy. In fact, the Chicken Noodle Soup recipe through step 5—minus the salt and the garlic clove—is exactly that. Making homemade chicken stock is worth it, particularly when the chicken stock is front and center, as it is in a soup.

My favorite way to make it is in my pressure cooker. The ingredients used in Chicken Noodle Soup, are too copious for the average pressure cooker, but if you halve everything, you can have home-made chicken stock in less than an hour, and it's always crystal clear. You don't even have to go to the trouble of the bouquet garni—you can just toss everything in the pot willy-nilly. Ohhhh, and I adore my pressure cooker, which reminds me . . .

How I Learned to Love My Pressure Cooker:

Everybody thinks that if you use a pressure cooker, it's going to blow up, probably in your face. It happens in the movies, after all—doesn't Audrey Hepburn explode her dinner in *Breakfast at Tiffany's*? Yes, the consensus is, if you own a pressure cooker, you're asking for it.

:CHICKEN SOUP
ADDITIONS:

To plain broth, add.

PARSLEY
–and
GARLIC
PUREE

BASMATI
RICE

CANNED
CHICK PEAS

TOMATO
PUREE

TOMATO

LEFTOVER
POT ROAST

Then I guess I am. I made JS get me a pressure cooker for my birthday (romantic, no?) and I was so excited I read the instruction manual before I went to sleep that night. The bottom line is, modern pressure cookers are scientific marvels and, if you are good and follow the directions, you can turn out all sorts of wonderful, long-cooked dishes in fractions of the time. So return that extra carrot juicer and get yourself a pressure cooker. You'll be OK, I promise.

Applesauce

*H*omemade applesauce is one of those things where there's no contest between the stuff in the supermarket and what you make at home. It's a great use of older apples, plus there's Pilates-esque repetitive exercise in turning the food mill, so you can skip the gym the day you make it.

3 lbs. cooking apples, such as McIntosh, Macouns, or Jonathans

¼ to ½ cup superfine sugar

Fresh lemon juice to taste (about ½ lemon's worth)

1. Wash the apples, cut them into quarters, and then throw them, seeds and all, into a large pot. Add ¼ cup water and turn up the heat to medium-high, covering the pot and cooking the apples until they're completely tender, about 30 minutes.
2. Fit your food mill over a bowl or another pot, add some apples to the bowl of the food mill, and start cranking. Keep going. Yes, some more. Whew. Think of the calories you're burning! I always feel very virtuous food-milling away.
3. When all the cooked apples have gone through the mill—the seeds and skins will stay behind—stand back and admire your work. Homemade applesauce has a lovely blush to it because of the fruit's skin. Taste it for tartness, then add a squeeze of lemon juice for brightness and a bit of the sugar to taste. Eat it right away, refrigerate it, or freeze it for the winter, as you prefer.

SPECIAL EQUIPMENT: *A food mill and someone who doesn't mind some upper-body exercise, like an Olympic rower or a steam-pipe fitter.*
TIME: *45 minutes*
FEEDS: *6 people, but you can increase this recipe as you like. It freezes perfectly.*

McINTOSH
- for sauce -

GALA
- for sautéing -

CRISPIN
- for pies -

ROME
- for eating -

JONAGOLD
- for baking -

NOT ON LOVE ALONE

FEBRUARY

The Atkins Counterrevolution

The Atkins Counterrevolution

I N THE SUMMERTIME, it seems reasonable to eat a piece of grilled fish with some hollandaise sauce and nothing else, waving away the bread basket, proud of your anti-carbohydrate willpower. But in the winter, when it's so dark and dreary, it becomes harder to withstand the allure of a nice plate of pasta or a hearty helping of mashed potato. Particularly those mashed potatoes. They're homey. They're filling. They're warm. They're better than anything else on the plate.

So in honor of falling off the Atkins bandwagon, I offer a humble but spectacularly good midweek February menu. It's basic and open to many interpretations; in fact, since any good home can't have just one potato recipe, I've provided three, along with a variety of winter salads and dressings to choose from, followed by several easy citrus fruitbased desserts. In its many permutations, it'll get you through any number of February snowstorms.

But February isn't all snow boots and down parkas; smack in the middle is that excuse for elaborately wrapped presents: Valentine's Day. So my Atkins counterrevolution continues in a small and sweet Valentine's menu as well.

Potatoes Three Ways

POTATOES ALIGOTE (PAGE 32)
POTATOES CRIQUE (PAGE 34)
ROASTED POTATOES WITH SHALLOTS AND TOASTED WALNUTS (PAGE 35)
&
WINTER SALADS AND A SELECTION OF
GOAT CHEESES (PAGES 36 AND 38)
&
SIMPLE CITRUS DESSERTS (PAGE 39)

True Love

DOUGHNUT BITES WITH CHOCOLATE GANACHE FILLING (PAGE 40)
&
CHAMPAGNE AND OTHER BUBBLIES (PAGE 42)

Potato Family Tree

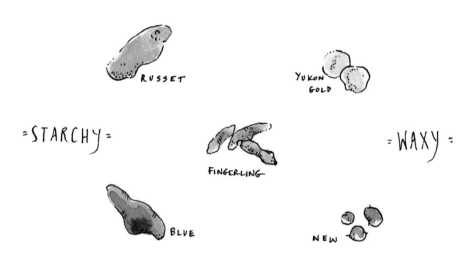

RUSSET

YUKON GOLD

= STARCHY =

FINGERLING

= WAXY =

BLUE

NEW

I T SHOULD COME as no surprise to hear that not all potatoes are created equal. Wait—that makes it sound as if I'm potato prejudiced. Perhaps I should say that all potatoes are special, in their own way.

Certainly you're familiar with the Idaho, or russet, potato, the floury giant of the tuber kingdom. High in starch, russets and their relatives are perfect for baking, deep-frying, and mashing.

On the other end of the spectrum, the basic white cooking potato is higher in moisture and lower in starch, giving it the sobriquet *waxy*. It's perfect for boiling and roasting. Though the white potato is humble, it counts among its cousins the very chic fingerling vari-etals, including Russian Banana Fingerlings and French *rattes*. Then there are new potatoes—so cute, but in fact they're just the imma-ture version of good old white potatoes.

In between, we find the golden mean of potatoes: Yukon Gold, the butter-colored, round variety that performs as well in starchy recipes as it does in waxy ones. Consider it a gift from the potato gods.

Then, of course, there are exotic potatoes, like purple potatoes from Peru, which make an intriguingly colored mashed potato and look great mixed in with other potatoes in a roast. Visit your local farmers' market in the fall for a crash course in unusual varieties. And if that doesn't scratch your potato itch, you can always airlift them in. Wood Prairie Farm (www.woodprairie.com), an organic potato farm in Maine, boasts a potato-of-the-month club for the true tuber fanatic.

POTATOES THREE WAYS

Potatoes Aligote

Despite your newlywed glow, yours isn't the first perfect marriage. Indeed, I contend that the first perfect marriage wasn't even between a man and a woman, but between a potato and a cheese—Potatoes Aligote, an old-fashioned French peasant food from a region called the Auvergne, located in the Massif Central.

1 generous lb. Yukon Gold potatoes

½ cup milk

4 tablespoons butter

½ lb. semisoft cow's-milk cheese, such as Laguiole, Cantal, or Tomme, cut into small pieces (you can also use Gruyère, Swiss, or fontina in a pinch)

Kosher salt and pepper, to taste

A healthy sprinkling of snipped fresh chives

1. Peel and quarter the potatoes, put them in a large pot of cold, salted water, and bring them to the boil. Boil until tender, about 15 to 20 minutes. Drain.
2. Remove the potatoes from the pot and, using a ricer (an essential and cheap kitchen implement for those who like potatoes), rice them back into the pot. (Alternatively, you can return all the potatoes to the pot and mash them with a hand masher.)
3. Meanwhile, heat the milk and butter in a small bowl in a microwave or in a small pan on the stovetop until the milk is hot and the butter has melted. This should only take a minute or two, either way.

4. Add the cheese to the potatoes and mix with a wooden spoon to melt—you may have to use minimal heat if the cheese isn't ripe and soft enough. Add the milk and butter, and heat some more. You can always add more cheese if it's not sufficiently cheesy—the *aligote* should have some elasticity to it. Add salt and pepper, amply.

5. Put the potatoes in a bowl and snip some chives over the top. Eat right away!

SPECIAL EQUIPMENT: *To make superlative mashed potatoes, all girls and boys need a potato ricer, but if you don't have one, it's OK just this once. Use a potato masher instead—just be sure and stay far away from your food processor, which makes potatoes unpleasantly gooey.*
TIME: *30 minutes*
FEEDS: *2 for dinner, 4 as a side dish*

Potatoes Crique

This recipe satisfies the desire for a bit of crunch with your potato. It's really a massive hash-brown, but with more delicate flavors, and is a specialty of the Ardèche region of France.

1 lb. russet potatoes, peeled	1 tablespoon chopped fresh chives
2 eggs, lightly beaten	Salt and pepper, to taste
3 tablespoons crème fraîche or sour cream	1 tablespoon unsalted butter, plus 1 tablespoon olive oil, for cooking
1 tablespoon chopped fresh flat-leaf parsley	Lemon wedges

1. Grate the potatoes on the largest hole on a box grater, or shred them in a food processor. Toss them in a bowl, and add the eggs, the crème fraîche, the herbs, and the salt and pepper, and stir.
2. Place the butter and the olive oil in a nonstick skillet or omelet pan and heat until the foam subsides. Put half of the potato mixture into the pan and press it down until it covers the whole bottom surface of the pan, forming a thin cake.
3. Cook the potatoes over medium heat until golden on the bottom, about 7 minutes, then *carefully* flip the cake over and cook on the other side (it can be useful to use two spatulas, like tongs). Though you want the potato to brown, make sure the heat is not too high, or the potatoes will be blackened before they're cooked through.
4. The large *crique* makes an impressive presentation, but if it's too much of a headache, you can make smaller ones. (If you make smaller *criques*, keep them warm while you finish cooking the remaining mixture by tenting them with aluminum foil or holding them in a 200°F oven. You will probably need to add a bit more olive oil to the pan as you proceed.) Cut into wedges and serve right away. I often like my *crique* with a squirt of lemon at the table.

TIME: *15 minutes*
FEEDS: *2 as a main course, 4 as a side dish*

NOT ON LOVE ALONE

Roasted Potatoes with Shallots and Toasted Walnuts

The flavors here are more robust than in the previous two potato recipes. While this is lovely as a main course, it does an excellent job alongside braised or roasted beef as well.

2 slices bacon

A drizzle of neutral oil (such as canola or safflower)

1 lb. fingerling or new potatoes, scrubbed

6 shallots, trimmed and cut in half if large

Salt and pepper, to taste

¼ cup whole walnuts

A handful chopped fresh flat-leaf parsley

Walnut oil (optional)

1. Preheat the oven to 400°F.
2. Snip the bacon into little matchsticks with your kitchen scissors. Throw the bacon in a roasting pan (big enough to subsequently hold the potatoes) with a drizzle of the neutral oil. Place the pan in the oven and let the bacon render for 5 minutes, then remove.
3. Toss the potatoes and the shallots in the fat in the pan. Add some salt and pepper to taste and toss again. Place in the oven and roast for 25 minutes. Pull the pan out of the oven again and sprinkle the walnuts over the top. Return the pan to the oven and continue to roast until the potatoes are golden brown and tender, the shallots have caramelized, and the walnuts are toasted, about 10 more minutes.
4. Pour into a serving dish, sprinkle with parsley, and toss with a few drops of the walnut oil, which becomes fragrant with the heat of the potatoes. Serve right away.

TIME: *About 40 minutes*
FEEDS: *2 as a delish dinner, but it's great as a side dish for 4 with, for instance, a roasted chicken (see page 138)*

Winter Salads

$\mathcal{I}$ N GENERAL, A big, leafy salad of Boston or Bibb lettuce, very lightly dressed, is my favorite sort of salad year-round. However, when the salad is part of the main course it's nice to have a bit more weight to it.

It's also important to be as seasonal as possible. Winter greens tend to be more bitter than their summer counterparts and so do well with a little sweetness: a julienne of Granny Smith apple, for instance, is lovely in an endive salad; some jarred chestnuts sautéed with shallots is delicious in a salad of frisée and red oak lettuce.

As much as I hate to say it (as salad washing and spinning is hands-down my least favorite kitchen task), you shouldn't buy those cellophane packages of prewashed lettuce if you can help it. Lettuce is always better carefully cleaned and dried at home. My preferred method is to lay out the clean leaves on a paper towel, then roll the leaves in the paper towel and store them in a zip-top bag in the fridge. That way, they stay crisp and fresh longer. If you can bear to do this right away with a head or two when you get home from the greengrocer's, you'll have lovely washed salad all week long.

Salad dressing is the hardest part of a salad to master. Lots of people overdress their salads, weighing the leaves down, or dress the salad too far in advance, making for a very soggy salad. Another pet peeve of mine is salad dressing that's too acidic or vinegary. Salad dressing is there to complement the ingredients of a salad, not to beat them into submission.

But in one respect salad dressing is the easiest part of a salad, as the best dressings have very few ingredients, and once you've developed a light touch, they are mixed more by taste than by measurement. I like a ratio of about 4:1 for oil to acid.

Some of my favorites: hazelnut oil, fresh lemon juice, salt and pepper; heavy cream, fresh lemon juice, salt, and pepper; garlic-infused olive oil, chopped fresh flat-leaf parsley, sherry vinegar, salt, and pepper; olive oil, a bit of Dijon mustard, sherry vinegar, fresh lemon juice, salt, and pepper.

I suggest trying any of the winter salads here with a small selection of goat cheeses (see page 38).

Winter Salad Combinations:

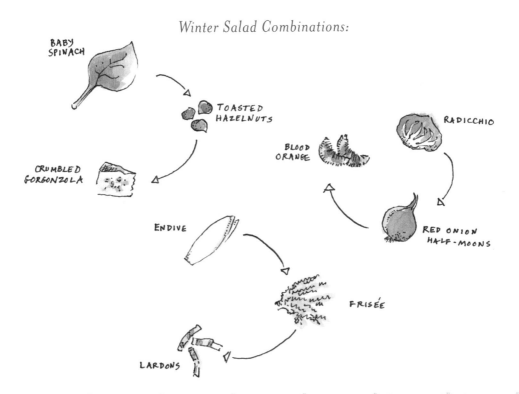

BABY SPINACH

TOASTED HAZELNUTS

CRUMBLED GORGONZOLA

BLOOD ORANGE

RADICCHIO

RED ONION HALF-MOONS

ENDIVE

FRISÉE

LARDONS

Fromage!
a Cheese Play in Five Acts

ACT ONE: *Chèvre, Mon Amour*

SCENE: *Murray's Cheese shop, corner of Cornelia Street and Bleecker Street, New York City. Daytime. J stumbles in, carrying large, unwieldy bag of groceries. CIELO stands behind the counter, cool as a cucumber.*

J, *wedging her bag between the Parmigiano Reggiano and the chorizo display.* Whew. Hi, Cielo. (*J examines the display case of cheese.*) Could I please have . . . (*Indecision sets in.*)

CIELO, *cheerfully.* Hello, lady. What are we making for dinner?

J. Oh, just some potatoes and salad . . . I dunno . . . maybe some goat?

CIELO, *gesturing toward the Selles-sur-Cher.* This is very good today. Nice, ripe. (*He forks over a sample.*)

J, *eating.* Mmmmm . . . (*She eats some more.*) Mmmmm, mmmmm . . .

CIELO. How much do you want, thirty pounds?

J. Yeah, but I forgot my wheelbarrow.

(black out)

CELLES - SUR - CHER

CHEVROT

MONTRACHET

TOMME de CHEVRE

CROTTIN

◡ SIMPLE CITRUS DESSERTS ◡

February: It's freezing. My socks are always wet from the slush puddles at the corners. It's pitch black at four o'clock in the afternoon. Is it any wonder that I get lost in Dickensian fantasies of decidedly Victorian illnesses I've suddenly contracted? I latch on to any chronic condition that sounds as if I'm in dire need of a fainting couch and a mustard plaster. Pleurisy? Lumbago? Consumption? Bring 'em on.

That's why citrus desserts are a good idea in February.

Vitamin C seems a worthy foe of all diseases Victorian, and citrus brings a sparkling brightness into a world gone into deep freeze. They need not be complicated; in fact, the closer the fruit remains to its original state, the better. And the preparation should take no longer than ten minutes, which should leave you just enough strength to crawl back to the fainting couch and eat dessert.

Some suggestions:

- ❧ Orange sections sprinkled with cinnamon

- ❧ Grapefruit sections roasted with brown sugar

- ❧ Orange sections with caramel sauce over vanilla ice cream

- ❧ Grapefruit sections and fresh mint, sautéed in butter and sugar, served over a dollop of mascarpone cheese

- ❧ Mixed citrus salad sprinkled with sugar and Grand Marnier

See Sectioning an Orange on page 101 for tips on preparing citrus fruit.

TRUE LOVE

You might notice a lack of dinner in this menu, but here's some good advice: nobody wants to do dishes after dinner on Valentine's Day. So do yourselves a favor and go out to eat, and save the dessert and some bubbly for later.

Doughnut Bites
with Chocolate Ganache Filling

Nice underwear . . . check; Champagne . . . check; mood lighting . . . check; doughnuts . . . check? I'm not talking Dunkin' Donuts here. These are tiny triangles of deep-fried dough filled with chocolate ganache, a very elegant bite for two to enjoy with a glass of Champagne.

You can make these doughnuts ahead and seal them in an airtight container for when you come home.

FOR THE DOUGHNUTS:

1 cup warm water

2 (¼-ounce) packets active dry yeast

3½ tablespoons superfine sugar

2 sticks butter, softened

5 large eggs

4 cups all-purpose flour

1 teaspoon salt

Neutral vegetable oil (such as canola or safflower) for frying

FOR THE CHOCOLATE GANACHE:

7 ounces semisweet chocolate

¾ cup heavy cream

1 teaspoon unsalted butter, softened

FOR DUSTING THE DOUGHNUTS:

Superfine sugar

1. Put the warm water, yeast, and a teaspoon of the sugar in a little bowl until the yeast wakes up—somewhere between 5 and 10 minutes. When you check the yeast, it should be nice and foamy.

2. In a medium-size bowl, cream together the butter and remaining sugar. When it's uniform, beat in the eggs, one at a time, and mix until completely incorporated. Add the flour, salt, and yeast mixture and mix on low until just combined. The dough will seem very slippery and loose—almost like a mistake—but don't worry, this is the way it's supposed to look. Cover the bowl with plastic wrap, put it in the warmest place in your kitchen, and let rise until doubled, about 2 hours.

3. After the dough has risen, punch it down, take it out of the bowl, wrap it in plastic wrap, and put it in the fridge for at least 3 hours.

4. Make the ganache: Chop the chocolate into slivers. Heat the heavy cream in a small saucepan until it's just scalding at the edges. Immediately take it off the heat and add the chocolate, stirring to combine. When it's smooth, drop in the butter and mix again. Set aside until thick, at least 30 minutes.

5. Pour 3 inches of oil into a deep saucepan (or follow the instructions on a deep-fryer) and heat it until it reaches 330°F (check it with a frying thermometer).

6. Meanwhile, take the dough out of the refrigerator and cut it into three portions. Wrap up the first two individually in plastic wrap and then put them in a freezer-safe bag; these can be defrosted and used when the fancy takes you. On a lightly floured counter, pat out the remaining portion into a square until it's about 1½ inches thick. Then, take a paring knife and cut off little triangular doughnuts, each side about 1½ inches long.

7. Carefully drop the doughnuts with your fingers into the hot oil and fry until golden brown. Remove them with a slotted spoon or bamboo-handled strainer and drain them on cookie racks placed over paper towels. While they're still warm, sprinkle them with superfine sugar.

8. If you have a pastry bag with a medium-size tip, fill it with some cooled ganache, poke a hole in the side of a doughnut with the tip, and pipe in a bit of chocolate. You can also poke a hole in the doughnut with a chopstick first and fill it with the handy zip-top bag method: fill a resealable bag with the ganache, then snip off one corner, so you have a ½-inch opening. Or, serve the ganache alongside the doughnuts, which is messier but just as good, and might fit in perfectly with the goals of the evening.

SPECIAL EQUIPMENT: *A hand mixer or standing mixer; a slotted spoon or bamboo-handled strainer.*
TIME: *At least a day, to let the dough rise, but much of that is unattended. You can also freeze this dough ahead of time and just defrost and fry the day of, about 30 minutes' work.*
FEEDS: *Each third makes about 16 doughnuts.*

Champagne and Other Bubblies

*J*S AND I HAVE a friend, Joyce, who has made a crucial lifestyle choice: when it's available to her (particularly if it's free, like at our wedding), she will drink Champagne, and only Champagne, until the last drop is gone. I wholeheartedly support her in this endeavor.

My father is a big believer in this Champagne principle as well, and I've come to believe that it's an inherited trait, as there's nothing more satisfying at the beginning of a dinner party than the pop of a pressurized cork. Having to pay for my own, however, I've learned that the lovely stuff my father drinks is usually out of my price range. My local wine merchant came to the rescue with some more reasonable selections. Here, a brief primer on the bubbly:

Champagne: Obviously the original, Champagne refers to the sparkling wine made in the Champagne region of France. It's an *appellation controllée*, which means that no one else can use the name, even if they use the same process for making sparkling wine, as the best California producers do. These are the wines in the famous bottles, the mustard-yellow Veuve Clicquot label, the Art Nouveau style of Perrier Jouët, or the antique-gold chevron of Dom Perignon. These are some of the more expensive brands, but you can get a perfectly tasty Champagne-style wine in the $30 range from producers like Lanson, Schramsberg (which is American, so technically a sparkling wine), and Moët-Chandon.

Prosecco: If Champagne and its California sparkling wine cousins are a little steep for your budget, Prosecco, an Italian sparkling wine, is a great alternative. Proseccos are young wines that have a crisp bite to them. They're particularly good in the summer, when you can make the great Venetian cocktail, the Bellini, from a mix of white-peach puree and Prosecco. Proseccos are very reasonably priced, in the $10–$15 dollar range.

Cava: Another very young sparkling wine, Cava is from Spain and is very similar to Prosecco, though it tends to be a little fruitier. It's also a more reasonably priced option, running you about the same as the Prosecco. Don't leave a bottle in your fridge for months and months, though, as the younger the Cava, the better it is.

March

A Fish Tale

A Fish Tale

ONE OF THE first things I learned about JS when we moved in together was that he had a fondness for fish sticks. And when I say fondness, I really mean obsessive love bordering on the unhealthy. He can eat an entire box in one sitting—which I'm sure is not the recommended serving size on the back of the package—and he doesn't even use tartar sauce. (Isn't that fish-stick sacrilege?)

While the occasional fish stick does send me on a Proustian journey to my days in the third grade, in general I'm wary of the industrially formed fish stick, in the same way I'm repelled but beguiled by that greatest of all mystery foods, the Chicken McNugget. Fish, particularly, is best when left alone, allowed to be itself with a minimum of human intervention. It was with this principle in mind that I conceived my first menu for this month.

It's a good thing to know how to cook fish properly, and it's not scary or hard. It just involves a bit of attention for a very short period of time. I've included a simple recipe for Fish Fillets Meunière, along with a green bean salad. You can serve the green bean salad as a separate first course, but I like to serve it alongside the fish, particularly in the spring and summer, when the cool crunch of the salad is a welcome counterpoint to the pan-hot fillet. I've also included my favorite ways to poach shrimp, steam mussels, and sear scallops, three versatile seafood dishes that are open to a thousand interpretations—if you follow a few rules.

So now, in between bouts of fish sticks, JS will indulge in a little well-cooked flounder or a steamed mollusk or two, prepared not by the Gorton's Fisherman but by yours truly.

Go Fish

GREEN BEAN AND HAZELNUT SALAD (PAGE 48)

&

FISH FILLETS MEUNIÈRE (PAGE 52)

&

LEMON GINGER TART (PAGE 54)

~

Seafood—The Greatest Hits Collection

BEST POACHED SHRIMP (PAGE 57)

&

BEST STEAMED MUSSELS (PAGE 58)

&

BEST SEARED SCALLOPS (PAGE 59)

GO FISH

Green Bean and Hazelnut Salad

I'm not crazy about hazelnuts in desserts—well, except for a dollop of Nutella now and then—but I absolutely adore them in savory dishes, particularly with green beans. You can get hazelnut oil at a gourmet shop and keep it in the fridge so your investment doesn't go rancid on you. It's a lighter, sweeter alternative to olive oil, but if you don't have it, don't fret—olive oil works just fine.

1 lb. green beans, trimmed (if you are having a dinner party, you could splurge for tiny *haricots verts*)

¼ cup raw hazelnuts

1 small shallot, minced

Small handful of fresh flat-leaf parsley, chopped fine

2 tablespoons hazelnut oil

Sea salt and pepper, to taste

1. Blanch the green beans: Put the beans in a shallow saucepan, cover them with cold water, and add a good pinch of salt. Bring them to a boil over lively heat until the beans are still firm but not crunchily raw, about 4 minutes, depending on the heftiness of your beans. The best way to test them is to taste them; alternatively, pick one up by its end and hold it horizontally. If it's ever so slightly relaxed (a small bend, not a total collapse), the beans are done. Drain and immediately run under cold water, tossing to cool them (this is very important if you want to keep them bright green).

2. While the beans are cooking, toast the hazelnuts. This is easily done in a few minutes in a 400°F toaster oven. Or you can swirl the hazelnuts in a dry, heavy-bottomed pan over high heat until they're fragrant and toasty. Either way, keep a close eye on them so they don't burn. Turn them out onto a cutting board and give them a medium-rough chop, removing any hazelnut skin that falls off (don't worry too much about this—it's more for aesthetics than anything else).

3. Put the cooled beans, hazelnuts, shallot, and parsley in a bowl with the hazelnut oil and toss to combine, adding salt and pepper to taste. It's best to keep this at room temperature if you're going to serve it anytime soon; if you want to store it overnight, it should go, covered, into the refrigerator.

TIME: *Less than 10 minutes; it can be made ahead and kept at room temper-ature for several hours*
FEEDS: *2 to 4 people*

⌇ VEGGIES & NUTS IN FRIENDSHIP ⌇

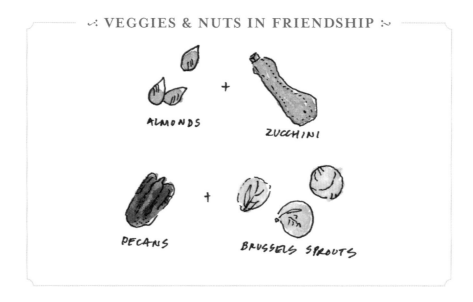

ALMONDS + ZUCCHINI

PECANS + BRUSSELS SPROUTS

A Trip to the Fishmonger

At any high-end supermarket or gourmet store, there's sure to be someone behind the fish counter who can help you make sense of the seafood buffet in front of you. I like to take JS shopping with me to my local fish store, Citarella's, because (a) he's very good at carrying packages, and (b) he's always astounded by the display. He thinks to ask the fishmonger questions I don't, such as "What the hell is a razor clam?" and "How do you cook rock shrimp?" and "Can you give me a slice of tuna so I can eat it raw right now?" (The answer to the last question was yes, by the way.)

The lesson here is *ask questions*. The people behind the counter are always happy to answer them, because they work with fish all day and have a bit of knowledge on the subject stored up. And fish can be tricky, as the same species might be called different things in different countries. So you might have had some provocatively named Loup de Mer at that snooty French restaurant, for instance, but you were just eating Sea Bass. (And if you suck up to the fishmonger enough, he might just give you free fish. Just ask JS.)

Special Fish Utensils:

Fish Fillets Meunière

A classic, easily made.

⅓ cup all-purpose flour

Sea salt and pepper

3 tablespoons butter

2 thin white fish fillets, such as flounder, gray sole, or cod (nothing that has a $24.99 per pound price tag)

1 tablespoon chopped fresh parsley

Lemon wedges for serving

1. Put the flour on a dinner plate close to the stove. Stir in the salt and pepper. In a nonstick sauté or omelet pan, heat 2 tablespoons of the butter over medium heat until the foam subsides. Dredge one fillet in the flour, then shake off the excess. Lay it in the hot butter, leading away from your body to prevent spattering fat, burns, stained shirts, et cetera. If your pan is big enough, repeat with the second fillet.

2. Cook over medium-high to high heat until golden, about 3 minutes per side. Be aggressive with the heat—if it's too sluggish, the fish will poach rather than sauté in the fat. You're aiming for a crunch on the outside, with the fish remaining creamy and tender inside. The trickiest part about this is regulating the heat— you don't want to scorch everything and burn the butter, but if the heat's too low, the fish will be greasy.

3. When the fish is finished, transfer the pretty fillets to a dinner plate. You'll notice that the butter in the pan has turned a lovely nutty brown. (You did it by accident, but the French call this *beurre noisette,* so be rightfully proud.) Turn down the heat to medium-low, add the remaining tablespoon of butter, and when it's melted, add the parsley. Spoon a tablespoon or two of the *beurre noisette* over each fish fillet. Serve with the lemon and a sprinkling of sea salt. Perfect.

SPECIAL EQUIPMENT: *Nonstick pan strongly recommended.*
TIME: *Less than 10 minutes*
FEEDS: *A pair of newlyweds*

NOT ON LOVE ALONE

Pastry Primer

∞

THERE ARE SEVERAL different types of pastry crust out there. The example in the Lemon Ginger Tart recipe is a modified *pâte sucrée*, which is really wonderful but a bit temperamental, like a purebred dog. There's also *pâte sablée*, which is a cookie crust, and the tried-and-true *pâte brisée*, which on this side of the ocean is just called plain old pie crust. You can make pastry crust with butter, with vegetable shortening, or a mix of both, but the fundamental ingredients are flour, fat, salt, and water.

There are two hard-and-fast rules: the shortening should be as cold as possible, and you should mix the dough as little as possible. Sounds easy, right? If only. The best way to be proficient in pastry is to practice. Then, if you think only good thoughts, meditate on world peace, and are kind to all children and animals, you can become Master of Your Own Pastry. We can all dream.

≡PASTRY ACCOUTREMENTS≡

ROLLING PIN

PASTRY CLOTH

PASTRY CUTTER

SCRAPER

Lemon Ginger Tart

This tart is a great favorite of mine, because I loooove a lemony dessert. The hint of ginger in the crust adds a bit of sweet heat that plays against the brightness of the lemons. Though I'm not going to tell you this is the fastest dessert in the world to make, there's something nice about being the Master of Your Own Pastry, even if it's not too pretty the first, well, dozen times you make it. Don't let that scare you! If you have a food processor, making this tart isn't very difficult. And making it in March is a particularly good idea, as the cooler temperatures make for cooler pastry-chef heads.

FOR THE PASTRY:

1 ¾ cup bleached all-purpose flour

4 tablespoons sugar

1 teaspoon ground ginger

pinch of salt

1 stick plus 1 tablespoon cold butter, in ½-inch cubes

1 large egg

¼ cup ice water

FOR THE FILLING:

2 lemons, washed

1 cup heavy cream

2 large eggs

2 egg yolks

½ cup sugar

pinch of salt

1. Lay a sheet of waxed paper on the counter. Put the flour, sugar, ground ginger, and a tiny pinch of salt in the bowl of your food processor. Pulse once to combine. Then add the cubed butter and pulse—in 1-second bursts—ten times, until the mixture looks like roughly ground cornmeal.

2. In a small bowl, beat the egg lightly. Add the egg and 1 tablespoon of ice water to the flour mixture and pulse twice to combine. If it's not coming together in a ball, add another tablespoon or two of water. It really depends on how humid the day is—a stickier day will give you stickier dough.

3. The moment the dough comes together, dump it out onto the waxed paper. Squish it into a ball, and roll it up in the waxed paper, and then in plastic wrap. Put it in your freezer if you have pressing time concerns, or in the fridge if you have all day.

4. If you put the dough in the freezer, let it chill at least an hour. If you put it in the fridge, let it chill for 3 hours.

5. Preheat the oven to 350°F. Take out the dough and let it sit in your warm kitchen for 5 minutes. On a floured surface, roll the dough out with a floured rolling pin, trying to keep it even in thickness, until you have a respectable circle that almost covers the bottom of your 9-inch pan. Then, draping the dough over a long spatula, transfer it to the tart pan and help it fill out the rest of the way by patting it in the pan, starting at the center and radiating out and up the sides of the pan. Not very pretty, but no one's going to see it anyway. Try to build up the sides a bit over the edge of the pan, since the crust will shrink slightly in baking. Prick it with a fork a few times.
6. Line your nice crust with parchment paper and place some dried beans or rice, or a fancier version of pie weights, in there. Bake until the edges of the crust are lightly golden, about 20 minutes. Take the tart shell out of the oven, remove the parchment (careful with the beans!), and let cool.
7. Turn down the oven to 325°F.
8. While the tart shell cools, make the filling. This includes one of my least favorite kitchen tasks, zesting lemons. But go ahead, zest them, then place the zest and the cream in a medium-size bowl and set aside.
9. Slice the pith (the white stuff) off your denuded lemons and throw away, as it's very bitter. Slice the lemons widthwise (be sure to remove any pits!).
10. Throw the slices in a blender (or your freshly washed food processor) with the eggs, egg yolks, sugar, and tiny pinch of salt. Blend.
11. Strain the mixture into the bowl with the cream and whisk until combined. Put the cooled tart pan on a cookie sheet so if there's any spilling, you won't have to clean the oven later. Pour the filling into the tart shell and carefully transfer it to the oven. Bake for 35 to 45 minutes, until the filling in the center jiggles just slightly when encouraged. Remove from the oven, let cool, and eat.

SPECIAL EQUIPMENT: *A food processor (plus a blender if you have one); a rolling pin (you could use a wine bottle as a substitute); a 9-inch tart pan (a removable bottom is an extra bonus); parchment paper; and pie weights, by which I mean a $1.39 bag of dried beans.*
TIME: *You'll need an afternoon, because the pastry has to rest after you make it. But lots of the time is unattended.*
FEEDS: *10, comfortably*

SEAFOOD—
The Greatest Hits Collection

ometimes the best things in life are the most difficult to cook. This is certainly true of shrimp, mussels, and scallops, all of which can be sublime if cooked properly but are often done in by some ham-handed chef. Think of that poor mussel, giving up its life to metamorphose into one of those rubber superballs you get out of a gumball machine. Or that sad sad shrimp that now seems to be made of damp recycled newspaper. Well, fret no more over our briny friends. Below I've included my three foolproof ways to cook shrimp, mussels, and scallops. The only rule is, please follow my rules exactly. And don't walk away from the stove.

❦ THINGS TO DO WITH POACHED SHRIMP ❧

OLIVE OIL
- and -
LEMON

- or -

PEA SHOOTS
- and -
SCALLIONS

- or -

RED ONION
- and -
CELERY SEED

Note: Fish Smell Be Gone! A small dish of vinegar placed in your kitchen after your fish feast will rid the room of any lingering aromas.

Best Poached Shrimp

I hate peeling shrimp. It's one of those painful kitchen tasks that has you sighing over the sink while you waste water and smell like a Japanese rice cracker. So I don't peel them—not right away, at least. I think you get better flavor if you cook the shrimp with their shells on, and I think they're easier to peel when they're cooked. Try it.

1 stalk celery, cut in half

1 medium carrot, peeled and cut in large chunks

1 medium leek, white and light green parts only, split lengthwise and carefully washed

2 sprigs fresh flat-leaf parsley

⅓ lemon

5 peppercorns

1½ teaspoons kosher salt

1 lb. large shrimp

1. Put the celery, carrot, leek, parsley, lemon, peppercorns, and salt in a 4- or 5-quart saucepan, and cover with 2½ quarts cold water. Cover the pot and bring the water to a boil over medium-high heat. When the water reaches the boil, take off the lid and let it boil happily for 10 minutes.

2. Meanwhile, rinse the shrimp under cool water (don't peel them). As the 10 minutes needed for the stock come to a close, set your kitchen timer for 2 minutes. Add all the shrimp to the water and, when the pot comes back to boiling, start the timer. As soon as the timer goes off, drain off the whole pot into the sink through a colander.

3. Give yourself and your fingers a minute before you begin the peeling and the cleaning of the shrimp, otherwise the suckers will be too hot. All you do is tear off the outer shell and the tiny legs, leaving the tail on. Deveining a shrimp then just means a quick incision down the back with a paring knife and a run under the faucet. The shrimp today is so clean already, anyway, there's practically nothing to remove.

4. If you're going to use the shrimp right away, keep them at room temperature rather than refrigerating them, because their texture is absolutely perfect right after poaching and refrigeration makes them a bit tougher. Poached shrimp can be served in a million ways; take a look at the sidebar for some ideas.

TIME: *25 minutes (mainly for peeling the shrimp)*
FEEDS: *Ample serving for 2 as a main course*

MARCH: A FISH TALE

Best Steamed Mussels

Mussels are quite inexpensive, but feel like a treat. I love mussels, but sometimes I find the broth turns a slightly unappetizing taupe color. To rectify this, I add a good pinch of saffron, which turns the liquid an appealing shade of Provençal yellow.

1½ lbs. mussels	2 sprigs fresh thyme
1 tablespoon unsalted butter	Pinch of saffron
1 tablespoon olive oil	Sea salt and pepper
3 shallots, sliced into rounds	¼ cup white wine

1. Rinse the mussels. Today's mussels are so clean that heavy-duty wrestling with beards and ugly barnacles is no longer necessary. Just throw out any mussels with broken shells and any fellows who, if open, won't close tight when encouraged by pressing the shells together for a few seconds. Run them under cold water in a colander and let drain. Keeping them submerged in fresh water will kill them (which you *don't* want to do).

2. Melt the butter with the olive oil over medium heat in a medium-size saucepan. When the butter's foam has subsided, add the shallots and sauté until there's some caramelization, about 5 to 7 minutes. Add the thyme, the pinch of saffron, a few grindings of pepper, and a pinch of salt. Stir for a minute or two more.

3. Turn up the heat to medium-high. Add the mussels all at once, then the little bit of white wine, and cover tightly. Keep the lid on for 3 or 4 minutes, then check the mussels. They're done as soon as they're gaping open, and you've got to get them off the heat right away, or you'll have little rubber erasers to eat instead of juicy mussels. Serve them in shallow soup bowls with an extra plate for the shells.

SPECIAL EQUIPMENT: *A medium-size saucepan with a tight-fitting lid*
TIME: *20 minutes*
FEEDS: *2 as a main course, 4 as a starter*

SERVE MUSSELS OVER TOASTED COUNTRY BREAD!

NOT ON LOVE ALONE

Best Seared Scallops

Scallops probably seem to shout out Special Occasion Only! but I always like making them for just the two of us. Cooking them up in small batches ensures the most precise cooking, and since they're done in a flash, you have no excuse but to make them rather than send for takeout.

2 strips of bacon, snipped into ¼-inch matchsticks

10 sea scallops, about ½ pound

Freshly ground pepper, to taste

Drop of olive oil

3 cups baby spinach, washed and dried

Small squeeze of fresh lemon

Sea salt, to taste

1. Heat a nonstick pan over medium-high heat and add the bacon strips. Render them, stirring, until they're crispy and have given up all their fat. Remove the bacon strips with a slotted spoon and let them drain on a paper towel.
2. Set your kitchen timer for 1 minute. Keeping the heat lively, sprinkle the scallops with some freshly ground pepper, then place them in the pan, one by one, as quickly as possible. When they're all in, start the timer. When it beeps, flip the scallops over, cover the pan, and restart the timer for 1 minute. When it goes off, transfer the scallops from the pan to two dinner plates.
3. Add a drizzle of olive oil to the hot pan and then add the baby spinach, giving it a few turns, until it just starts to wilt. Mound the spinach next to the scallops, add a tiny squeeze of lemon and a sprinkling of sea salt, and then toss a few bacon bits on top and serve.

SPECIAL EQUIPMENT: *A nonstick pan with a lid is a lifesaver here.*
TIME: *10 minutes*
FEEDS: *2 for dinner*

Wine for Fish

𝒥 ALWAYS LIKE A light, crispy white wine, such as a Sancerre or a nice dry Riesling, with white fish or shellfish, because it doesn't overpower the delicate flavors. Of course, I always like a Sancerre or a nice dry Riesling, even with microwave popcorn or a Snickers bar. But I still think you should try them with the fish.

APRIL

Early Birds

Early Birds

W HEN JS AND I go to the green market at Union Square early on Saturday mornings in late April, the farmers are just starting to get in a few local spring vegetables. Instead of the usual complement of carrots, beets, and old sweet potatoes, we begin to see hints of the bounty to come: ramps and spring garlic, for instance, or the beginnings of a few strawberries here and there.

Of course, some of the most evocative springtime vegetables don't find purchase in Hudson River Valley farms in April, but come to NYC from sunny California. My favorite of these is the artichoke, available year-round but best in the early spring, which is its actual season. In the first menu I've included both artichokes and another spring favorite, asparagus. The other elements are the best, tenderest pork roast you'll ever eat, and an old family recipe—a chewy, featherweight meringue cake bolstered by whipped cream and strawberries.

Speaking of old family recipes, early birds are often hungry after foraging at the green market and carrying their purchases twenty blocks and up five flights of stairs. On my mother's side, I am the happy inheritor of dozens of old-fashioned Pennsylvania Dutch breakfast recipes, three of which I give here. There's nothing chic or trendy about these dishes—which is what makes them so good.

Spring Forward

HERB-BRAISED ARTICHOKE HEARTS AND PEAS (PAGE 64)

&

ROASTED ASPARAGUS (PAGE 65)

&

PORK LOIN BRAISED IN MILK (PAGE 68)

&

NONNA'S WRONG WAY TORTE (PAGE 72)

Mom vs. Aunt Debbie

NANNY'S APPLESAUCE CAKE (PAGE 76)

NANNY'S SCOTTISH CREAM SCONES (PAGE 77)

NANNY'S CINNAMON STICKY BUNS (PAGE 78)

SPRING FORWARD

~

Herb-Braised Artichoke Hearts and Peas

Braised artichokes are delicious but somewhat muted in color. When you add the peas at the very end, they add a nice punch of green.

¼ cup olive oil

6 artichokes, prepped (see Conquering Artichoke Hearts, page 66)

1 clove garlic, slightly crushed but still in one piece, peeled

½ cup mixed chopped fresh flat-leaf parsley and mint

¼ cup chicken stock

Kosher salt and freshly ground pepper, to taste

1 cup high-quality frozen peas

Good crusty bread for serving

1. In a heavy-bottomed saucepan with a tightly fitting lid, heat the olive oil until shimmering. As it's heating, cut the artichoke hearts into quarters. Once the oil is hot, add the garlic clove and let it cook until fragrant, about 30 seconds. Then add the artichoke hearts.
2. Swirl the hearts around in the oil, then add all the parsley and mint, plus the chicken stock. Give it a good pinch of kosher salt and a grinding of pepper, then cover the pot, turn the heat down to low, and let the artichokes cook for 20 minutes.
3. At the end of 20 minutes, test the hearts for doneness (the tip of a paring knife should slide right through them). If you're satisfied, throw in the peas (if you can find fresh peas, you can use them instead—if you use them the day you buy them. Otherwise fresh peas get really mealy really fast). Put the lid on for a minute or two more, so that the peas heat through and get some of the herb flavors. You can serve this hot or at room temperature, but whatever you do, serve it with plenty of crusty bread to sop up all the sauce.

~

TIME: *1 hour, including a leisurely whittling down of the artichokes*
FEEDS: *6 as a side dish or a first course*

Roasted Asparagus

A quick and flavorful springtime dish.

1 lb. asparagus, trimmed	3 tablespoons olive oil
Zest of ½ lemon	Sea salt, to taste
3 tablespoons fresh flat-leaf parsley	

1. Fill a large, deep-sided skillet partway with salted water and bring it to a boil. Add the prepared asparagus and blanch for 2 minutes, then immediately drain and run under cold water to stop the cooking. Alternatively, have a large mixing bowl of ice water standing by in which to plunge the blanched asparagus.
2. Preheat the oven to 500°F.
3. Toss the blanched asparagus with the lemon zest, parsley, and olive oil. Sprinkle on some sea salt to taste. Lay out the asparagus on a rimmed cookie sheet. Place the sheet in the oven and roast the asparagus for 5 to 7 minutes, or until the buds just start to turn color but the stalks remain a vibrant green. Remove from the oven and serve immediately, or at room temperature.

TIME: *15 minutes or more, depending on how fancy you get with the asparagus (see Prepping Asparagus, page 71)*
FEEDS: *6 as a side dish*

Conquering Artichoke Hearts

RTICHOKES ARE DELICIOUS—but daunting at first. We ate them all the time growing up, but I never paid much attention to how to cook them, so when, as a teenager, I finally looked them up in Julia Child's *Mastering the Art of French Cooking*, I was surprised to find it involved a lot of lemon juice and yards of cheesecloth. Talk about a production.

Since then, I've boiled them, I've steamed them, I've fried them, I've braised them. JS is still partial to an artichoke at room temperature with a simple vinaigrette to dip the leaves in, and there's no more preparation needed than snipping off the tips of the daggerlike leaves and boiling them in acidulated water (this is where the lemon juice comes in) for 30 to 40 minutes.

But to get to the, er, heart of the matter, carving up an artichoke is a bit more complicated.

1. First, remove the bottom three rows of leaves, snapping them backward and pulling them off. Rub this naked area with the cut side of a lemon half.

2. Then, with a large chef's knife, slice off the entire top part of the artichoke, right down to the point where you've denuded the thing. Cut off the stem entirely. Rub the whole thing with the lemon.

3. Using a paring knife—or even better, a boning knife, which is longer and very flexible—begin to carve away any green from the bottom and any evidence of leaves from the top of the artichoke heart. You will be left with a lightly chartreuse, potato-firm disk about an inch and a half thick and 4 inches in diameter.

4. Now to tackle the worst part, the needlelike choke. This can get a bit

messy, so do it over a bowl on your workspace or over the garbage can. Inserting the tip of the paring knife in the flesh of the artichoke just below the edge of the choke, cut in a circular motion to lift the choke out in one piece. The idea is to save as much of the heart as possible while ridding yourself of the inedible choke. Toss the quills and rub again with lemon. You've survived!

THE ELUSIVE HEART of the ARTICHOKE

YOU NEED:

ARTICHOKE   LEMON   BIG KNIFE   SMALL KNIFE

CUT OFF THE TOP...

...SLICE OFF THE STEM...

...PULL OFF THE REMAINING LEAVES...

...PARE OFF REMAINING GREEN BITS...

...SCOOP OUT THE CHOKE WITH A SMALL KNIFE OR SPOON...

...DOUSE WITH LEMON.

TADA!

Pork Loin Braised in Milk

This is a very traditional Italian dish that sounds a little curious before you try it. The principle is very simple, and the major ingredients are two: a pork loin and milk. You can experiment with flavoring the milk, adding lemon peel, or sage, or more garlic than I've done here, but I recommend keeping it simple, because this pan sauce, though a bit homely, is one of the tastiest in the world.

One more note: I make this dish with half-and-half because modern pork is bred very lean and therefore the sauce can use the extra milk fat. But you can certainly get delicious results using whole milk instead.

2 tablespoons unsalted butter

1 tablespoon neutral vegetable oil (such as safflower or canola)

Salt and pepper

3-lb. piece of pork loin, weighed with the ribs still attached, then de-boned and tied, with the bones included (or a 2½-lb. pork loin roast, with a ½ lb. portion of pork short ribs or a small rack of baby back ribs)

1 clove garlic, crushed and peeled

Bay leaf

3 cups half-and-half

Good, crusty bread or basmati rice, for serving

1. Heat the casserole over medium-high heat, and add the butter and vegetable oil. (The bit of vegetable oil will keep the butter's milk solids from burning.) Salt and pepper the pork loin and the ribs, then add the pork loin to the pot and give it a good crusty browning, probably about 12 to 15 minutes total. Regulate the heat if, despite precautions, the butter is looking a little dark. When you're satisfied with the golden goodness of your pork, take the loin out and put it on a plate. Set it aside for a moment.

2. Drop the ribs in the pan and begin to brown them, along with the garlic clove and the bay leaf. When the ribs have gotten a little color, return the loin to the pot. Add 1 cup of the half-and-half, bring to a boil, then cover the pot and turn the heat down to the barest minimum.

3. You should turn the pork every 20 minutes or so, for even cooking and to see how the sauce is progressing. After an hour, the half-and-half will have cooked down quite a bit, forming a rich, butter-colored, custardy sauce. Add another cup of half-and-half at this point, bring it back to a

boil, then cover it again and turn the heat back down to a minimum. Continue to check it every 20 minutes (as Yogi Berra said, "It's déjà vu all over again").

4. At the end of 2 hours, take a state of the union. The pork should be nearing completion, which in this case means moist and easily pulled apart with a fork. The sauce should be mostly boiled down again. Add another ½ cup of the half-and-half (you can add part or all of the remaining ½ cup if you think the pot looks dry). Cook for half an hour longer, this time with the lid slightly ajar. When the pork is perfectly tender, take it out and place it on a platter. Lift out the ribs—these are the treat for the chef. Tilt the casserole and spoon off some of the excess fat that might have collected on top of the thickened half-and-half. Fish out the bay leaf and the garlic clove, if you can find it. If the sauce isn't as thick as you like, you can cook it down over moderate heat for a few minutes more, but not for too long or you run the risk of scorching it.

5. Slice the pork into ½-inch-thick rounds, then serve it with a healthy dollop of the pan sauce on top, with the basmati rice or crusty bread on the side.

SPECIAL EQUIPMENT: *The only thing you really need for this is a high-quality casserole with a heavy-duty bottom, such as a Le Creuset, that will fit the pork snugly.*
TIME: *At least 3 hours, but remember your mother always said that good things come to those who wait. And besides, you can go on with your life while you cook, since it's largely unattended.*
FEEDS: *6 lucky souls*

Bringing Home the Bacon

BACK AT OTTOMANELLI'S, Frank is always particularly patient as I hem and haw about what I want for dinner. Pork loin is more of a special-event dish, so that gets nixed. Pork tenderloin is delicious cut into medallions and sautéed with a mustard sauce, but that's too involved for tonight. Maybe a pork shoulder, other- wise known as a Boston butt, would be good, braised in white wine and herbes de Provence . . . but . . . actually I think I'll just take some bacon and make some BLTs.

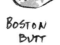

BOSTON
BUTT

RIB ROAST,
BONE IN

PORK
TENDERLOIN

AND OF COURSE
BACON

Prepping Asparagus

∞

Asparagus is a breeze. It's such a breeze that sometimes I have JS clean it while I'm doing other things. Basically, asparagus already knows how far to trim itself. If you hold one end of the spear in each hand and gently start to bend it, it will snap at the perfect place. Snapping off a bunch of asparagus takes, oh, a minute and a half. I rarely bother to peel the bottoms of the snapped spears on your average Tuesday night, but if I were looking to impress I would.

SNAP off The ENDS

THEN PEEL!

Nonna's Wrong Way Torte

This recipe is the result of a terrible, terrible mistake. My paternal grandmother, Nonna, often made this cake, the happy results of an ancient family recipe her mother misread, accidentally inverting the amount of flour and sugar. It's a sort of pavlova with a gooey, sugar-cookie crust and it has lasted a lot longer than the original version, I can assure you.

½ cup vegetable shortening, such as Crisco, plus extra for greasing the pans

½ cup all-purpose flour, plus extra for dusting the pans

1 cup sugar

4 egg yolks and whites, separated

1 teaspoon vanilla extract

1 teaspoon baking powder

¼ teaspoon salt

¼ teaspoon cream of tartar

1 cup superfine sugar

2 pints strawberries, washed, drained, and hulled

1 pint heavy cream

1. Preheat the oven to 250°F. Prepare the springform or standard cake pans: First, rip off a sheet of parchment that's larger than the bottom of the pan, and, using a pen, trace the circumference of the bottom of the pan onto the paper. Cut it out just inside that line. Repeat. Then, liberally grease the pans with vegetable shortening, particularly in the corners, and flour them. Lay a round of parchment in the bottom of each prepared pan, and grease and flour the parchment. (This preparation might seem a bit baroque, but this dough redefines sticky, so the baked cakes can be quite recalcitrant when it's time to take them out of the pans.)

2. In a mixing bowl, cream the sugar with the ½ cup vegetable shortening. Add the egg yolks and blend, one by one. Add the vanilla, then sift in the ½ cup flour, the baking powder, and the salt. Divide the mixture in half and press each portion into the bottom of a pan. You'll have to do some work to stretch it from edge to edge—it sometimes helps to dampen your fingertips a bit while you do this, so the dough won't stick to them. It will be a very thin layer of dough, like a cookie.

3. Put the egg whites in the impeccably clean bowl of a standing mixer, or use a hand mixer. Start on low speed, breaking up the albumen in the egg whites, then add the cream of tartar and bring the mixer up to speed, until you have stiff peaks. Then, at first by tablespoons, then in a thin stream, add the superfine

sugar and beat until you have a glossy, thick meringue. Spoon the meringue on top of the thin dough layers. Put the pans in the oven.

4. Bake the tortes for 25 minutes, then increase the temperature of the oven to 325°F and bake for 12 to 15 minutes more. This will give the meringue a golden top. Take the pans out of the oven and let cool completely before you remove the cakes from the pans. To do this, cut around the sides of each pan with a sharp paring knife, making an effort to get all the way to the bottom. Sometimes a bit of prying is necessary, but the parchment should save you from major heartbreak. Remember: be patient and wily. You will best the springform.

5. Prepare the strawberries by slicing them thinly lengthwise. Keep a few of the prettiest ones to decorate the top. Store in the refrigerator until needed.

6. Right before you're ready to serve, whip the cream into nice firm peaks. (It's always a good idea to chill the empty mixing bowl in the freezer until you're ready to start whipping the cream. It helps the cream set up.)

7. To assemble the torte, place one layer, meringue side up, on a serving plate, then cover the top of the layer with most of the whipped cream and most of the berries. Cover with the other layer, also meringue side up, and add a dollop of whipped cream to the top, along with the remaining sliced berries and the few whole strawberries you saved. A serrated knife is the easiest way to cut this precarious confection, which will fall apart anyway but—as we've learned in life—tastes just as good no matter what it looks like.

SPECIAL EQUIPMENT: *Two 9-inch round springform pans would be a bonus with this recipe, but two 9-inch round cake pans will do in a pinch. You will also need some parchment paper. A standing mixer or electric hand mixer is useful as well.*

TIME: *A bit more than an hour from start to finish, but the layers can be made ahead of time and assembled with the whipped cream before serving*

FEEDS: *At least 8, but people will always want seconds*

A Note on Eggs

BUY ONLY LARGE eggs. They're the standard eggs for any recipe. It will make your life easier.

And when you're separating egg yolks from egg whites to make a meringue, don't get any yolk in the egg whites by accident. If you do, you won't get anywhere with those egg whites. Ever.

OSTRICH

JUMBO CHICKEN

LARGE CHICKEN

DUCK

QUAIL

⌐ USE THIS EGG IN
≡BAKING≡ and ≡COOKING≡

MOM VS. AUNT DEBBIE

On my mother's side I have some Pennsylvania Dutch blood, which not only enables me to put a Pennsylvania Dutch Hex on any baseball team in danger of beating the New York Mets, but also makes me a keeper of the Pennsylvania Dutch Baking Flame. Mom and her cousin Deb (aka "Aunt Debbie") are guardians of generations of traditional recipes and techniques handed down from their grandmother, Nanny.

The only trick is that you need a clairvoyant to understand Nanny's recipes. The aged notecards say things like, "Mix the usual ingredients" and "Bake in moderate oven 'til done," and they're sometimes less than specific about amounts, methods, et cetera. Mom and Aunt Debbie both have opinions about what these cards mean, and sometimes the opinions diverge. In the battle of Mom vs. Aunt Debbie, however, I think Aunt Debbie wins. Aunt Debbie is an avid baker who even makes her own homemade dog biscuits, and Mom is a person who "retired" from cooking in 1992.

Nanny's Applesauce Cake

This is deeply spiced, as many old-fashioned recipes are, and perfect with a cup of coffee. You can make it, wrap it well in plastic wrap and foil, and freeze it to defrost at a later date.

1¾ cups all-purpose flour, plus extra for dusting the loaf pan

1 teaspoon ground allspice

1 teaspoon grated nutmeg

¼ teaspoon ground cloves

½ teaspoon salt

1 teaspoon baking soda

1½ teaspoon ground cinnamon

½ cup butter, softened (keep the wrapper for greasing the loaf pan)

¾ cup sugar

1 egg

1 cup applesauce

1. Preheat the oven to 350°F. Grease and flour a standard loaf pan.
2. Sift together the first seven ingredients, through the cinnamon, into a small mixing bowl. In a larger bowl, cream together the butter and sugar until smooth, then add the egg and mix until combined. Add the applesauce and mix—it won't look very smooth, but don't worry about it.
3. Gradually add the flour mixture and stir until combined. Pour the batter into the prepared loaf pan and bake for 50 to 55 minutes, or until a toothpick inserted in the center comes out clean.
4. Let the cake cool completely in the pan, then wrap it tightly in plastic wrap. It's so spiced it's perfect plain, and even better the next day.

SPECIAL EQUIPMENT: *A 9 x 5-inch loaf pan*
TIME: *1 hour*
FEEDS: *You could get 10 nice slices out of a loaf.*

NOT ON LOVE ALONE

Nanny's Scottish Cream Scones

My Aunt Debbie told me that my Grandma Baker, Nanny's daughter, put three stars by this recipe on her recipe card. I don't think any further explanation is necessary. Except this: don't overmix the dry and liquid components. And by don't overmix, I mean barely mix at all. Think of all the bricklike scones you've choked down at bridal shower teas in your life, and you'll heed well my warning.

5 tablespoons butter, chilled and cut into ¼-inch cubes, plus a bit of softened butter to grease the cookie sheet

2 cups all-purpose flour

1 tablespoon sugar

1 tablespoon baking powder

½ teaspoon salt

½ cup half-and-half

2 eggs, lightly beaten

1. Preheat the oven to 425°F. Lightly grease a cookie sheet.
2. Sift together the dry ingredients into a mixing bowl, then cut in the chilled butter using a pastry cutter, two forks, or (my preference) your own two hands.
3. Mix together the half-and-half and the beaten eggs, then add the egg mixture to the flour mixture. Mix very gingerly, just until combined. The cardinal rule here is, the less you touch your dough, the more tender your scones will be.
4. Turn the dough out onto a well-floured pastry cloth or a well-floured board. Pat the dough together—try not to knead it at all—then cut it in half with a floured knife. Form each half into a 6-inch round, then cut each round into four pieces. Place them an inch apart on the prepared sheet and bake until golden, about 12 minutes. They come out light and fragrantly eggy. If you can, eat them hot with butter and a robust jam, such as raspberry or blackcurrant; they taste best the day you make them.

SPECIAL EQUIPMENT: *A pastry cloth, if you have it*
TIME: *About 30 minutes*
FEEDS: *8, if each person eats only one scone (not likely)*

Nanny's Cinnamon Sticky Buns

$\mathcal{I}$ saved the best for last. This recipe card, when I first looked at it, was particularly cryptic, referring to mysterious "fruit" that went inside. As I never remembered my mother putting any fruit in these, we had a talk. "I think she would put candied fruit in it," said Mom, "but I put pecans in instead." So while it might be inauthentic, I'm recommending the Virginia Carry variation here.

Nanny's treatment of the yeast was also a bit vague. Mom's helpful suggestion? "Call your Aunt Deb in Cleveland."

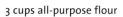

¼ cup warm water

¼ cup plus ½ teaspoon sugar

1 (¼-ounce) package active dry yeast

5 tablespoons unsalted butter, plus some to grease the baking pans

1 egg

½ teaspoon salt

1 cup whole milk

3 cups all-purpose flour

⅔ cup light brown sugar, plus 1 cup for sprinkling

½ cup raisins (I like golden ones)

⅔ cup pecan halves

1 teaspoon ground cinnamon

4 teaspoons molasses

1. In a small bowl, mix the warm water, ½ teaspoon of the sugar, and yeast. Set it aside to start to come to life and foam, about 5 minutes.

2. In the bowl of a standing mixer, cream 3 tablespoons of the butter with the remaining ¼ cup sugar until smooth. Add the egg and beat until combined. Add the salt, then the yeast mixture (your mixer should be on a very low setting), then the cup of milk. Slowly add the flour, a cup at a time, and mix until the whole dough is completely combined. Stop the mixer, scrape down the sides, then turn the whole mess (it's very slippery and sticky) into a bowl you've greased, maybe with the wrapper from the butter you just used. Cover the bowl with plastic wrap. Set the bowl someplace warm and let it rise for 2 to 3 hours, or until it has doubled in volume.

3. When the dough is ready, prepare two 9-inch round cake pans by liberally greasing them with vegetable shortening or butter. Don't skimp here or you'll have a headache later. Sprinkle ⅓ cup brown sugar over the bottom of each pan and set aside.

NOT ON LOVE ALONE

4. Generously flour the surface where you plan to roll out the dough. Flour your hands, then coddle the dough into deflating, finally turning it out onto the work surface. Remember, flour is your friend here. Dust the top of the dough, cut it in half, and move one portion to the side to deal with in step 7. As best you can, pat, press, and pull the dough into a rectangle about 10 inches by 8 inches. If you've ever played with pizza dough, that's how this dough behaves—if it springs back, coax it into shape.

5. When you've done your best, sprinkle the top—making an effort to cover the whole surface—with ½ cup brown sugar, ¼ cup raisins, ⅓ cup pecans, and ½ teaspoon cinnamon; dot it with 1 tablespoon of the butter. Roll it as best you can from one long edge to the other, like a jelly roll. Then cut it into 1-inch rounds. You should get eight or nine rounds.

6. Place the rounds, touching, cut side up around the rim of one of the prepared cake pans. Cover it with greased plastic wrap and let it rise again at room temperature for 2 hours.

7. Repeat steps 4 through 6 with the second pan (you could also use one larger pan), then clean up the immense mess you've made of your kitchen. Or better yet, guilt your significant other into doing it by going on about the delicious cinnamon sticky buns you're making.

8. Preheat the oven to 350°F.

9. Drizzle the tops of the buns with the little bit of molasses, just for some added depth of flavor. Pop the pans in the oven and bake for 25 minutes, checking after 20. They're done when they're golden brown and have formed a cake in the pan. Pull them from the oven, and immediately upend them onto a serving platter. Wait 5 minutes before devouring them or you'll burn yourself on the hot sugar.

SPECIAL EQUIPMENT: *A standing mixer is useful here, though I doubt Nanny had one. A pastry cloth is also useful for rolling out the dough. Two 9-inch cake pans.*

TIME: *At least 4 hours of unattended time, as you must wait for the dough to rise twice; the actual mixing and baking takes 40 minutes.*

FEEDS: *This recipe makes about 16 sticky buns.*

MAY

Déjeuner sur l'Herbe

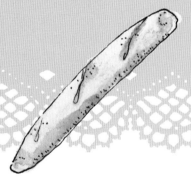

Déjeuner sur l'Herbe

As a kid, I was not a champion picnicker. Ants grossed me out. Bees made me panic. I could never get the hang of planting my glass in the grass so that it remained upright instead of dumped on my lap. As an adult, however, I love to picnic, particularly in the spring. It might have something to do with the fact that, by spring, JS and I have been cooped up in our tiny Greenwich Village apartment (it was advertised as having "Parisian charm," which is code for no bathtub) for well on four months, and look as sickly and pale as downtrodden characters in a Dickens novel.

Picnicking is not something one does well right away. It involves some advance planning, some good luck, and a willingness to improvise. But the ultimate success of a picnic is up to you. Pack carefully. Choose your location wisely. Hide any open wine bottles inside your basket. Read the weather report. Oh, and have a good time. To facilitate your success with the latter, I'm offering a pretty foolproof picnic menu.

And when a full-blown picnic is not in the cards, there's still nothing to stop you from dining alfresco on a park bench. So when you want that picnic feeling without the picnic heavy lifting, consider one of my sandwiches—all very delicious and all very forgiving because they're mayonnaise-free.

Picnic Perfect

FRIED CHICKEN, SORT OF (PAGE 84)

&

FRENCH POTATO SALAD (PAGE 87)

CUCUMBER SALAD (PAGE 88)

&

PINWHEEL COOKIES (PAGE 90)

Picnic on a Park Bench

MINI PAN BAGNA (PAGE 93)

&

IMITATION OLIVE'S SANDWICH (PAGE 94)

&

LE SANDWICH MIXTE (PAGE 95)

PICNIC PERFECT

⌒

Fried Chicken, Sort of

*O*K *. . . this isn't real fried chicken. Real fried chicken involves very careful regulation of large amounts of extremely hot fat. Often the breast meat ends up as dry as can be. In this recipe, you poach the chicken first, so the frying at the end is really just window dressing. One more thing: though I call for a whole chicken so you get both white and dark meat, you could just buy an equivalent weight of thighs and drumsticks and avoid the chance of dry breast meat altogether.*

1 quart whole milk

4-lb. chicken, cut into 10 pieces
(see note)

2 cloves garlic, peeled

Bay leaf

1 generous pinch kosher salt,
plus 1 generous pinch

Neutral vegetable oil (such as canola or
safflower), for frying

2 cups all-purpose flour

1 teaspoon cayenne pepper (or to taste)

1. Put the milk in a saucepan and add the chicken, garlic cloves, and bay leaf, along with a hefty pinch of salt. Add a cup of water if the chicken isn't fully covered by the milk. Bring the saucepan to a slow simmer over medium heat and cook until the chicken is tender, about 15 minutes for the white meat and 20 for the dark (you can fish the breast pieces out and set them aside while the dark meat finishes cooking). Give the pot a stir from time to time to prevent any sticking.

2. When the chicken is done, turn off the heat and let the chicken sit tight for a minute while you heat the oil and prepare the flour mixture. Put a clean, dry skillet on the stove (a cast-iron skillet, if you've got it), and add enough vegetable oil so that it comes ⅓ inch up the sides of the pot. Turn the heat on to medium-high.

3. Combine the flour, cayenne, and a big pinch of salt in a zip-top bag, seal, and shake it like you mean it. Then open the bag and add a few pieces of the chicken (you can skin it if you like; in fact, I recommend skinning the breast pieces, as the skin will have shrunk during the poaching) and shake it to coat the pieces well. The oil in the skillet should be shimmering with the heat now, so lay the

chicken pieces gently in the oil, always aiming away from your body so as to avoid personal injury and loud, sustained cursing. Then, fry the chicken until suitably golden brown, flipping with tongs, about 4 to 5 minutes per side. You might want to do this in batches to avoid crowding the pan (which leads to soggy, not crispy, chicken). When the chicken is golden brown, remove it from the oil and let it drain on a cookie rack placed over a few pieces of paper towel or old newspaper. Let it cool to room temperature before packing it in your picnic basket.

NOTE: *If you buy chicken from the butcher, ask him to cut it up for you (the breast should be in four pieces total). If you buy chicken from the supermarket, get one package of thighs and drumsticks, and a split breast on the bone. When you're home, halve each split breast width wise.*

SPECIAL EQUIPMENT: *Most important is a good set of tongs and a skillet for frying the chicken—cast-iron would be superlative.*
TIME: *45 minutes, if you're zippy*
FEEDS: *4 picnickers*

Picnic Basket Absolutes

I'VE LEARNED EVERYTHING I need to know about picnicking from Anne Mackenzie-Stewart, a close family friend who happens to be from Edinburgh, Scotland. The Scots are hearty picnickers, despite the fact that the weather in Scotland often leaves a bit to be desired. There's even a joke: Where do you have a Scottish picnic? In the car.

So Scots come prepared for all eventualities. Here are some of the must-haves Anne always carries in her basket:

French Potato Salad

*There's no salad that reminds me so much of lunch in the fresh air as this one.
It has the perfect mix of creaminess and freshness.*

2 lbs. fingerling potatoes, or other little potatoes like tiny Yukon Golds (red new potatoes should be your last choice)

2 tablespoons Dijon mustard

2 tablespoons sherry vinegar or red wine vinegar

Sea salt and pepper, to taste

¼ cup olive oil

¼ cup mayonnaise

2 teaspoons fresh thyme leaves (or a whole sprig)

2 shallots, peeled and thinly sliced into rounds

1. Scrub the potatoes and place them in a large pot—a 4-quart pot should do the trick. Add cold water to cover the potatoes by at least 2 inches. Turn the heat to high and bring the pot to a boil, add a pinch of salt, and cook the potatoes until they're tender but not crumbling, between 15 and 20 minutes, depending on their size and freshness. They're done when the tip of a paring knife is easily inserted into their middles. Run them under cold water to bring the temperature down more quickly.

2. Meanwhile, in a bowl big enough to hold all the potatoes, mix the Dijon mustard and vinegar with a fork or whisk until completely combined. Add some sea salt and pepper to taste, then, in a slow, steady stream, whisk in the olive oil. You should have a lovely, mustardy vinaigrette. Then, add the mayonnaise and mix to combine. Add the thyme, the shallots, and the cooled potatoes—you can cut some in half, and leave others whole, as you like. Then taste and correct for salt and pepper. Serve right away, or cover and keep in the fridge until you're ready to eat it. It's best made as close to picnic time as you can, but it's fine spending the day in the fridge.

TIME: *About 20 minutes to cook the potatoes, plus a few minutes to let them
cool and dress them*
FEEDS: *4 as a side dish*

Cucumber Salad

ool and crunchy. A picnic favorite.

2 medium English (sometimes they're called hothouse) cucumbers

3 tablespoons rice wine vinegar

1 teaspoon toasted sesame oil

1 tablespoon chopped fresh mint leaves

Sea salt and freshly ground black pepper, to taste

1. Peel the cucumbers (you can peel them so they're striped green lengthwise) and slice them in half lengthwise. Using a teaspoon, scoop out any seeds—English cucumbers are much less seedy than regular old cucumbers. Slice each half crosswise into crescents, about ⅓ inch thick.

2. In a bowl that can hold all the cucumbers, mix together the rice wine vinegar, toasted sesame oil, chopped mint, a healthy pinch of sea salt, and several grindings of pepper. Add the cucumbers and toss until combined. Let sit at room temperature for at least 30 minutes, to allow the dressing to sink into the cucumbers (you can probably achieve this in the course of packing up the salad and toting it to your picnic spot).

TIME: *How long does it take to peel and slice a cucumber?*
FEEDS: *4 as a side dish*

∴ OTHER PICNIC SALADS ∾

CHERRY TOMATO

BASIL

MINI-MOZZARELLA

RED CABBAGE

CARROWAY SEEDS

LEMON JUICE

CELERY

EDAMAME

PARSLEY

≡ JUST ADD OLIVE OIL ^and^ VINEGAR ≡

NOT ON LOVE ALONE

Fromage!
a Cheese Play in Five Acts

ACT TWO: *Have Cheese, Will Travel*

SCENE: *A Saturday in late May, lunchtime. J and JS enter Murray's Cheese shop.
J is carrying a blanket over her arm. JS is carrying a large cooler, a giveaway from a
Mets game circa 1995. CIELO stands behind the counter, small smile on his face.*

J. We're going on a picnic. We need unmessy cheese, please. But
nothing too hard to slice.

CIELO. Hello, lady. Hello, man. (*He reaches over the
counter and gives JS a slice of cheese.*)

JS, *eating with an almost religious fervor*. Mmmmmm . . .
we'll take that . . .

CHEDDAR

CIELO. That's Taleggio. (*He forks over some more cheese to JS.*)
And this is a Cantal . . .

JS. OK, some of that, too . . . (*He peers into the display case dreamily.*)
What's that? I want some of that one there.

CIELO. That's a nice cheddar from Ireland. (*He smiles devilishly.*)
Anything else, man?

J, *interrupting*. See you later, Cielo. I think three cheeses are plenty for a
two-person picnic.

(*black out*)

CANTAL

TALEGGIO

Pinwheel Cookies

These are a great picnic option—and more original than brownies or chocolate chip cookies—because while they're chocolate flavored, they won't melt and coat your hands, picnic blanket, utensils, et cetera, with chocolate.

1½ cups all-purpose flour	1 egg yolk
½ teaspoon salt	3 tablespoons milk
½ teaspoon baking powder	½ teaspoon vanilla extrace
½ cup butter, softened (keep the wrapper for greasing the cookie sheets)	1 ounce (one square) unsweetened baking chocolate, melted
½ cup sugar	

1. Sift together the flour, salt, and baking powder into a small bowl.
2. In a food processor or with a hand mixer and a large bowl, cream the butter and sugar together; then (through the spout, if using a processor) drop in the egg yolk, followed by the milk and vanilla. Stop the machine and scrape down the sides of the bowl.
3. Add the flour mixture in four portions, blending after every addition. Up-end the bowl onto some waxed paper, and pat the dough into a ball. Divide the ball in half, put one portion back in the food processor bowl, and blend in the melted chocolate. Wrap the dough in separate sheets of waxed paper, then in plastic wrap (and further in tinfoil if you're going to freeze it at this point). They should sit in the fridge for at least 2 hours.
4. On a lightly floured board or pastry cloth, roll the vanilla layer out into a rectangle that's about 6 inches wide and 12 inches long. Carefully move it aside, then repeat with the chocolate layer. Put the chocolate layer on top of the vanilla, lining up the rectangles as well as you can. Then roll them up together lengthwise, as tightly as you can, so you end up with a long, thin cookie log. Wrap the log in plastic wrap and chill for another 30 minutes.
5. Preheat the oven to 350°F and lightly grease two cookie sheets. Unwrap the chilled cookie log and, using a very sharp knife and a light touch, slice into ¼-inch-wide slices. Place the cookies 1 inch apart on the prepared cookie sheets, and bake for 7 minutes, checking them after 5. They're done just after they set—

NOT ON LOVE ALONE

they shouldn't be browned at all. Transfer the baked cookies to a cookie rack and let cool. You can store them in a tin or another airtight container for several weeks.

SPECIAL EQUIPMENT: *A food processor makes life easier, and a pastry cloth is useful, but not necessary, to roll out the dough.*
TIME: *The dough needs to be refrigerated for several hours after it's made, but you can make it well in advance and freeze it, defrosting it overnight in the fridge. A single-day total would be 3 hours, mostly unattended.*
FEEDS: *The yield here is about 30 cookies. (I never make assumptions about how many cookies a single person can eat in one sitting.)*

PICNIC ON A PARK BENCH:
Eating alfresco every day

always feel a bit deprived if I don't have a sandwich for lunch. Sometimes I have a salad, but even with a heaping handful of croutons, I'm always grumpy afterward, thinking that everyone who had a sandwich is luckier than I am.

I also like making my lunch and taking it with me, particularly in the spring when I can sit in the park and raise my face to the breeze and munch on a sandwich and watch the city go by. May is when all the crazy people come out of hibernation, so there's a lot to watch.

So I would say, with all due modesty, that I'm a sandwich expert. I've included three recipes for sandwiches that are mayonnaise-free, so all those times you tempted fate by eating that soggy baloney and cheese on camping trips won't come into play here. These sandwiches won't kill you—they'll only make you stronger.

Mini Pan Bagna

Basically a Niçoise salad on a bun. Pack some breath mints along with an extra paper napkin for this one.

½ clove garlic, minced

¼ cup good olive oil

A drizzle of red wine vinegar

Sea salt and pepper

Sturdy, crusty sandwich roll (round or rectangular is better than baguette-shaped here)

1 (3.5-ounce) can of imported Italian tuna

1 small shallot, chopped

½ teaspoon capers, chopped

1 tablespoon chopped fresh flat-leaf parsley

A few black cured Provençal olives, pitted and sliced

1 hard-boiled egg, thinly sliced (optional)

1 small tomato, sliced

Several leaves romaine lettuce

1. In a small bowl, mix the garlic with the olive oil and red wine vinegar. Add some salt and pepper, then set aside.
2. Cut the roll in half and take out some of the soft insides from both the top and the bottom, creating a little bowl for the sandwich filling to sit in.
3. Drain the tuna, then flake it into another small bowl, mixing it with the shallot, capers, chopped parsley, and salt and pepper.
4. Using a teaspoon, drizzle the insides of your sandwich roll with the garlic-oil mixture. Then layer on the tuna fish, olives, sliced egg, tomato, and romaine lettuce. Put the top on the sandwich and give it a good smushing-down. Double-wrap it in plastic wrap, put it in a zip-top bag, and then put it in your bag to take to the office (or wherever you're headed).

TIME: *10 minutes*
FEEDS: *This is the floor model sandwich. Multiply it as many times as you like.*

Imitation Olive's Sandwich

his sandwich, another salad on bread (in this case, Caprese salad), is an imitation of a sand-wich I used to buy at college in a local shop called Olive's. I'd buy a sandwich, an oatmeal cookie, and some water, and sit on the large green in the middle of campus and laugh at the students trudging into the library.

A traditional French baguette

A sprinkle of good balsamic vinegar

Good olive oil

Sea salt and pepper, to taste

1 very ripe tomato, sliced

A ball of fresh mozzarella, sliced (ideally you should get the sort that comes swim-ming in water)

Fresh basil leaves, rinsed and patted dry

Small red onion, peeled and sliced into very thin half-moons

1. Cut the baguette in half. Drizzle each side with a touch of balsamic vinegar and some olive oil. Sprinkle with salt and pepper.
2. Layer the tomato, mozzarella, a few basil leaves, and a few half-moons of red onion on the bottom of the baguette, then top the sandwich with the other half of the bread. Slice in half, so you have two sandwiches. If you're taking it with you, be sure to wrap it in a double thickness of plastic wrap.

TIME: *5 minutes*
FEEDS: *2, if you use the whole baguette*

NOT ON LOVE ALONE

Le Sandwich Mixte

This is the sandwich you can get at any café in France, or at the airport after you've picked up the rental car and are trying to fit six bags in the trunk of the Economy Compact you've paid for. Deceptively simple, the sandwich's strength is in the quality of its ingredients.

A good crusty baguette

Good unsalted butter, softened

A few slices of cooked ham, such as *jambon de Paris* if you can find it

A handful of shredded Gruyère cheese or some thin slices of ripe Brie

Freshly ground pepper

1. Cut the baguette in half and slather each cut side with butter. Then layer in the ham if you can find it and the cheese. This sandwich should not be overstuffed, so a thin layer of each is perfect. If you use Brie, you might want to remove most of the rind, as it can be a bit chalky and distract from the perfection of this ham-and-cheese sandwich.
2. Cut in half, wrap in plastic wrap or waxed paper, and see if you can wait for lunchtime.

TIME: *The fastest sandwich of them all*
FEEDS: *2, if you use the whole baguette*

Summer Pantry

THOUGH I GAVE you some ideas for a basic pantry in the introduction, I want to mention some items I always have on hand in the summer. Most of these are picked up in my routine visits to the green market at Union Square. Though not strictly pantry items, these are building blocks to all good improvised summertime meals:

Tomatoes: Kept on the counter, not in the fridge.

Fresh herbs: All varieties, particularly parsley, basil, mint, and thyme, washed, wrapped in paper towel, and kept in the fridge in resealable bags.

Green beans: For salads of all sorts.

Zucchini: For salads, pasta, and frying.

Cucumbers: For salads and yogurt sauces.

Stone fruits: Such as small plums, for eating out of hand or baking.

Blueberries: There's always a pint in my fridge.

Lettuces: Washed, spun dry, and stored wrapped in paper towel and sealed in a zip-top bag.

NOT ON LOVE ALONE

JUNE

Midsummer and Midnight

Midsummer and Midnight

BEFORE I MARRIED JS my mother took me on vacation. We didn't end up in West Palm Beach. Instead, Mom packed me on a plane and off we went to Morocco, spending time in Casablanca, Marrakech, and camping (if you can call a tent with carpets on the floor "camping") in the Sahara.

As usual, I became obsessed with the food. In Morocco, eating is highly structured and ceremonial, and one of the points of pride in a Moroccan household is to make way too much food so that your guests will be impressed by the bounty. I ate salads and couscous, tagines and roasts, and began to get very interested in figuring out how to do it myself. When I got home, I started to do some research. While I've made some very authentic dishes (I've actually purchased a *couscoussière*, the proper pot for steaming couscous), I've also played around with Moroccan flavors in a less serious way, making dishes inspired by, but in no way true to, the Moroccan tradition. So with this in mind I'm giving you a faux-Maroc menu this month.

This vacation coincided with JS's bachelor party, held in sunny Jamaica. (Since I was riding a camel in the desert at the time, I forgot to worry about the collective maturity level of ten twentysomething males on vacation. I think they drank gallons of Red Stripe, and went cliff-diving at midnight—things I'm glad I didn't know at the time.)

One thing you might want after cliff-diving at midnight, however, is a snack. Though every nutritionist tells you not to eat after six o'clock at night (who can do that?) the midnight snack is alive and well in our household. Sometimes, it's as simple as JS downing two or three bowls of cereal after *The Daily Show* (JS often treats cereal like a *digestif*—we'll come home from a restaurant and, instead of a Cognac, he'll have Captain Crunch). At other times, you need something more substantial, like the recipes here. I fully guarantee that they'll make happy midnight snackers of you.

Mock Moroccan

COUSCOUS SALAD WITH CARROTS,
PINE NUTS, AND ORANGE (PAGE 100)
&
LAMB TAGINE WITH LEMON AND OLIVES (PAGE 104)
&
LEMON GINGER COOKIES (PAGE 108)

Midsummer Night Snack

RICE PANCAKES (PAGE 112)
&
POP'S GRILLED CHEESE (PAGE 113)
&
RELAXED BLUEBERRIES AND VANILLA ICE CREAM (PAGE 114)

MOCK MOROCCAN

Couscous Salad with Carrots, Pine Nuts, and Orange

The complementary tang of orange, sweetness of carrot, and smokiness of cumin really work well together. They've been incorporated into couscous here, which is not a very Moroccan thing to do at all, but still very good.

4 medium carrots, peeled and trimmed

1 cup chicken stock

½ teaspoon light brown sugar

½ teaspoon ground cumin

Pinch of ground cinnamon

1 tablespoon unsalted butter

Sea salt

1 cup dry couscous

1 orange, peeled and sectioned

¼ cup pine nuts, toasted

¼ cup chopped fresh flat-leaf parsley

¼ cup chopped fresh cilantro

1 tablespoon white wine vinegar

3 tablespoons olive oil

Pinch of hot pepper flakes

1. Cut the carrots on the bias into ¼-inch-thick coins, and put them in a frying pan with the chicken stock, brown sugar, ground cumin, cinnamon, butter, and a healthy pinch of salt. Bring to a boil over high heat, then turn down the heat to medium-low and cook for 15 minutes, stirring very occasionally. At the end of 15 minutes, turn up the heat to medium and boil away the remaining broth—the evaporating broth will glaze the carrots and intensify the flavors of the spices. This should take 10 minutes. When the carrots are done, turn off the heat and set the pan aside to cool.

2. In a bowl that's large enough to hold all the ingredients, mix the couscous with 1 cup of boiling water. Cover the bowl with plastic wrap (or another bowl) for 10 minutes, then fluff the couscous with a fork. Add the sections of orange, pine nuts, parsley, cilantro, vinegar, olive oil, and pepper flakes, and then the car-

rots, scraping out the pan well in order to get all the lovely glaze into the salad. Mix all the ingredients carefully with a spatula, then season with salt—it might need more than you think. I like to serve this with the tender inner leaves of a head of Boston lettuce, which give a lovely crunch and contain the couscous salad prettily inside their curves.

TIME: *45 minutes*
FEEDS: *6 as a side dish*

❧ SECTIONING AN ORANGE ❧

ANY CITRUS FRUIT is easily sectioned. Just cut off the stem end and bottom end so the fruit stands up, then, using a paring knife (or a boning knife, which is thin and flexible and thus perfect for this job), slice the rind off in sections. Trim off any leftover pith, then, holding the orange in your hand, carefully remove the sections in between the membranes.

Marinades, with a Touch of the Exotic

∞

MARINADE IS A great way to get a feel for more obscure flavors without committing yourself to a full meal extravaganza, and, in general, marinades are a great way to brighten up supermarket chicken breasts or flank steak. Frankly, these marinades are my equivalent of Old El Paso taco mix. They might not be too authentic or sophisticated, but they taste pretty good.

I always mix everything in a resealable bag and throw the bag out when I'm done, solving the problem of cleanup and refrigerator space at the same time.

1. *Pan-Asian marinade:* This might be the fakest of them all. Put a 1½-lb. piece of flank steak in a gallon bag, and follow that with 1 tablespoon rice vinegar, 1 tablespoon Thai fish sauce, 3 tablespoons soy sauce, ¼ teaspoon Thai chili paste, 2 crushed garlic cloves, and 2 sliced scallions. No need for salt, because the soy takes care of that. Marinate at least an hour before grilling or broiling.

2. *North African marinade:* Sometimes I marinate quails in this in the summertime and then grill them. Put a split chicken breast (on the bone, please) in a gallon zip-top bag with 2 teaspoons toasted whole cumin seeds, 2 crushed garlic cloves, ½ lemon

(squeezed, then tossed in), a good pinch of hot pepper flakes, ¼ cup olive oil, and a hearty pinch of salt. Marinate for ½ hour in the fridge, then broil those babies.

3. *Faux Greek marinade:* This marinade is based completely on tzatziki sauce, which is what douses your souvlaki at summer street fairs.

   In that same old resealable gallon bag, mix a split chicken breast on the bone with a 6-ounce container of Greek yogurt, 2 tablespoons of chopped fresh dill, the juice of ½ lemon, 3 crushed and chopped garlic cloves, and a pinch of salt. Marinate for ½ hour in the fridge, then broil. As in tandoori chicken, the yogurt really tenderizes the meat.

Lamb Tagine with Lemon and Olives

The name **tagine** *comes from the vessel these stews are cooked in—a glazed ceramic dish, with a long, dramatically curved funnel-shaped lid with a steam vent in the top. It looks a bit like a volcano. You can get the same flavors, however, in a casserole on your stovetop, even if you don't get the same theatrical presentation.*

Lamb tagines are often a bit sweet—one of my favorites is made with lamb and dried figs. But here I've opted for a version with the most basic of Moroccan flavors, lemon and olive.

3 tablespoons olive oil

Kosher salt and pepper

2 lbs. boned leg of lamb, extra fat trimmed, cut into 1½-inch pieces (this makes a firmer stew; if you want softer meat, but more pronounced lamb flavor, get the equivalent amount in boned lamb shoulder)

3 cloves garlic, minced

1 medium red onion, chopped

1 tablespoon freshly grated, peeled ginger

Pinch of saffron threads

1 teaspoon ground paprika

1½ teaspoons ground cumin

A few stems of fresh flat-leaf parsley (leaves removed) and one or two cilantro stems, tied together with kitchen string

1 cup pitted green olives, such as picholines

1 lemon, zested and reserved for juicing

1 egg yolk

2 tablespoons sheep's-milk yogurt or Greek yogurt

¼ cup chopped fresh flat-leaf parsley

Crusty bread for serving

1. In a casserole that can subsequently hold all the ingredients, heat the olive oil over medium-high heat until shimmering. Salt and pepper the lamb, then brown (in batches if necessary) until deep and caramelized on all sides. Be sure to get good color here. Remove the lamb to a plate with a slotted spoon and set aside.

2. In the fat, sauté the garlic until you smell it, then add the chopped onion and give it a good stir, cooking until it's translucent, 3 to 4 minutes. Add the ginger, and cook for a minute more. Then add the saffron, paprika, and cumin, and stir so everything in the pot is evenly distributed. Put the lamb and its juices back in the pot, add the stems of parsley and cilantro, and cover with 1½ cups of water. Bring to a boil, cover the pot, and turn down the heat to the barest minimum.

3. Check the lamb after an hour. With the lid slightly ajar, cook it for 15 minutes more, adding a tablespoon more of water if it's looking very dry.
4. Fish the lamb out and put it on a platter for a moment. Discard the limp parsley and cilantro stems. To the juices left in the pot, add the olives and the lemon zest. Stir to combine. Turn off the heat.
5. In a small bowl, whisk together the juice of half the lemon, the egg yolk, and the yogurt, then add it to the juices in the pan, stirring quickly to incorporate. Taste for salt and pepper. Add the lamb back to the pan, turning it in the sauce. You can heat this over the lowest of heats, but don't let it boil, or the egg yolk will curdle and separate. Sprinkle with the chopped parsley, and serve with crusty bread.

SPECIAL EQUIPMENT: *A casserole pot, such as the enameled cast-iron Le Creuset*
TIME: *30 minutes of work time, plus 2 hours of unattended stewing*
FEEDS: *6*

Lamb Cuts

*A*T OUR WEDDING we served a 1950s favorite, rack of lamb. There's something so elegant about the labor-intensive frenched racks being carved apart, and the rosy round of meat connected to the delicate bone propped on your plate. There's also something so wonderfully barbarian about sitting in your easily stainable pristine white wedding dress and fighting for the last bits of meat off the bone with your fingers and teeth. That's what bridesmaids are for—to help you clean up afterward.

RACK
of
LAMB

At Ottomanelli's, there are three cuts of lamb that I might choose from on an everyday basis. The first would be a few lamb chops; though the most expensive, I still think their flavor is the best. Sometimes Jerry will give me a portion of a leg of lamb, boned, and that's delicious, too, roasted with chilis and garlic in the oven—though that's a bit more special-event, to be honest.

LEG
of
LAMB

Then there are lamb shanks, which can be braised in Italian flavors or North African flavors, and there is lamb shoulder, which needs to be ruthlessly trimmed (it's very fatty) and used for stews like lamb with white beans or the lamb with vinegar and green beans that's in Marcella Hazan's famous book *Essentials of Classic Italian Cooking*.

Just ask the butcher—there's a world beyond the lamb chop, and it can be very tasty, indeed.

LAMB
SHANKS

Moroccan for Intermediates

THINK I'VE already mentioned that I own a *couscoussière*. I've actually opted to make couscous the crazy way (it involves several steamings, some massaging, and some drying—it sounds like a facial), rather than the sane way, which is to pour hot water in and cover for 10 minutes.

I have also (and I'm a repeat offender here) preserved my own lemons, which by rights should have been included in the tagine recipe on page 104. This involves slitting lemons with a razor blade, submerging them in brine, and storing them in your refrigerator for at least a month.

There's also a dish called the *pastilla* (it can be spelled fourteen different ways), which involves stewing pigeons and constructing an elaborate, pizza-size layered pie out of phyllo dough. There's a simpler chicken version of it as an hors d'oeuvre on page 208.

So you see, there's a bit of madness involved in becoming more deeply committed to cooking in any one style. Just like a person who has invested in several woks and some obscure Chinese condiments, I've paid my dues to the Moroccan food club. If you're interested in learning more about more traditional Moroccan food, I suggest you peruse Paula Wolfert's *Couscous and Other Good Food from Morocco*, a bible of Moroccan specialties and traditions.

Lemon Ginger Cookies

This is a much bastardized, very inauthentic Moroccan cookie. There are a lot of absolutely delicious cookies in North African cuisine, but they are tricky to make and involve things like homemade almond paste, rose water, and lots of powdered sugar.

These are a mite easier, but very cute and strongly flavored with lemon and ginger, a favorite combination of mine.

2 cups all-purpose flour

1 teaspoon baking powder

½ teaspoon baking soda

½ cup vegetable shortening, such as Crisco

½ teaspoon salt

½ teaspoon freshly grated lemon zest

½ teaspoon freshly grated nutmeg, or jarred grated nutmeg in a pinch

1 cup sugar, plus extra for rolling the cookies

2 eggs, lightly beaten

2 tablespoons milk

4 tablespoons well chopped candied ginger

¼ cup golden raisins (or ¼ cup slivered blanched almonds)

1. Preheat the oven to 350°F. Grease two cookie sheets.
2. Sift together the flour, baking powder, and baking soda into a small bowl or a large piece of waxed paper.
3. In a mixing bowl that can subsequently hold all the ingredients, use the hand mixer to cream together the vegetable shortening, salt, lemon zest, nutmeg, and sugar until smooth. Add the eggs. In increments, and on low speed, add the flour mixture. This is quite a stiff dough and you will end up with a face full of flour if you're not patient with the hand mixer.
4. When all the flour has been combined, mix the milk into the dough with a wooden spoon. Fold in the chopped candied ginger.
5. Scoop out dough in heaping teaspoons, roll into balls, then give the balls a quick spin in a plate of sugar. Put them on the baking sheet, make an indentation in the top of the balls with your finger, and put a golden raisin in the spaces. (Or,

if you prefer, a slivered almond.) Be sure to leave at least 1½ inches between balls because they will flatten out in the oven.

6. Bake for 8 to 10 minutes, or until lightly golden at the edges. Transfer to a cookie rack to cool, then store in an airtight container.

SPECIAL EQUIPMENT: *An electric hand mixer is useful but not a requirement.*

TIME: *About 10 minutes to make the dough, and 10 minutes to bake the cookies*

FEEDS: *The yield here is about 4 dozen. Previous caveats about cookie consumption apply.*

Spice Jar Roulette

I<small>T'S</small> OK. I<small>T</small> happens to all of us. A promising herb or spice, used once (and in a minuscule amount), haunts your spice rack for years. You refuse to throw it out on the principle that it's wasteful to do so, and besides, it cost you $8.49 in 1999.

I know. Mine is a jar of juniper berries, purchased once upon a time to flavor a stew, and ignored ever since. I have nothing against them . . . it just never occurs to me to use them.

But, in order to keep your jar of cumin in the rotation, why don't you use it on roasted cauliflower or butternut squash? You can always rub a cheaper steak with a bit of paprika and ground Jamaican allspice before you grill it. You can cook a cardamom pod or two with rice to perfume it, or color that same rice with a bit of bright yellow turmeric. Those caraway seeds can be toasted and tossed with cooked carrots or sautéed red cabbage. Resurrect that ground mace by tossing a pinch of it on pumpkin and squash before roasting. There's a world beyond dried thyme—you just have to figure out ways to explore it.

MIDSUMMER NIGHT SNACK

The cleverness of a midnight snack is directly proportional to how much leftover food you can use in making it. Old pasta? Some old grilled steak? Half a bowl of butternut squash soup? Put on your thinking caps.

In general, your late-night taste buds are looking for three things: salt, fat, and sugar. And since you know that what you eat after midnight doesn't count calorie-wise, you can go to town! In all seriousness, these three recipes are much better tasting and better for you than a drive-thru Big Mac.

⌒

✑ FAVORITE THINGS TO EAT AT 2 AM ✑
an Informal Poll

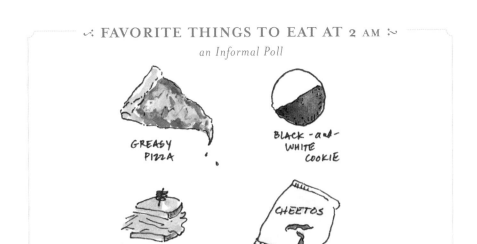

GREASY PIZZA

BLACK -and- WHITE COOKIE

HALF -a- TURKEY SANDWICH

CHEETOS

Rice Pancakes

This is a Carry family tradition, served to the kiddies for dinner on the occasional Sunday. Now I serve them to JS. While they cook, they start to smell like the best popcorn ever. They're crispy and creamy. They're salty and sweet. They might just be the world's most perfect food.

1 egg

1½ cups cooked rice (such as leftover Chinese take-out rice)

Small pinch of kosher salt, optional

1 tablespoon unsalted butter, plus more for serving

Maple syrup

1. Beat the egg lightly in a medium-size bowl, then add the rice and squish it with a fork to combine. Add the pinch of salt if the rice is unsalted.
2. Heat a nonstick skillet over medium-high flame, and melt the tablespoon of butter. When it's melted, add the rice in large spoonfuls and press them down a bit so they look like pancakes. Give them 3 or 4 minutes a side, until they're lightly golden.
3. Give your rice pancakes a bath in maple syrup (and a pat of butter, if you like) and eat up.

TIME: *You'll be eating by 12:10 AM*
FEEDS: *2 late-night snackers*

Pop's Grilled Cheese

This is actually a rainy-day vacation lunch, but it translates equally well to late-night snacking. The best part about late-night snacking is that you use as few utensils and pans as possible, and those you do use, you hide in the sink and clean the next day. It's guilt-free cooking.

Leftover country bread, sliced relatively thin (if it's a large loaf, slice each piece in half, and count that as a slice; these should be small sandwiches)

Some shredded Swiss cheese (or whatever sort of cheese you have hanging around)

Some ham from the lunch-meat drawer of your fridge

1 tomato, thinly sliced

Butter for frying

1. Heat a skillet over medium-high heat.
2. Just like regular grilled cheese, slather the butter on the outside of the bread, then layer a combination of the ingredients, to taste, inside. Because of the choice of bread, these can be a bit precarious in the pan—it helps to corral them with both a spatula and a fork when it's time to turn them.
3. Cook until golden brown on each side, then slide out of the pan and onto a plate or a paper napkin. Hunger cured.

TIME: *10 minutes*
FEEDS: *It depends on how many sandwiches you make!*

Relaxed Blueberries and Vanilla Ice Cream

This recipe calls into action a late-night friend: the microwave.

1 pint blueberries

2 or 3 tablespoons sugar

Squeeze of fresh lemon juice

Pinch of ground cinnamon

Vanilla ice cream

1. Rinse the berries, then put them in a microwaveable bowl with the sugar, lemon juice, and cinnamon. Using a fork or the back of a spoon, give them 3 or 4 mashes to break up a few of the berries. Microwave on high for a minute, or until the blueberries just begin to relax—this definitely depends on the strength of your microwave.

2. Take them out, give them a stir, then spoon them over the ice cream. Depending on what you have on hand, you could use frozen yogurt, regular yogurt (Greek is particularly good), leftover mascarpone cheese, or cottage cheese instead.

SPECIAL EQUIPMENT: *Your microwave*
TIME: *Merely a minute*
FEEDS: *2 late-night grazers*

NOT ON LOVE ALONE

JULY

Vacation, All I Ever Wanted

Vacation, All I Ever Wanted

MY PARENTS ARE major Francophiles. In fact, since my father retired, they spend nearly half their time in France, in a house they own in a village in the middle of the boondocks. Of course, the French have a nicer term for "boondocks"—they call it *la France profonde*. What that really means is that there are more goats than people.

Needless to say, it's quite a change from the big city, but they are very happy there, and we (by whom I mean me, JS, and my brother, Will) are very happy to visit them. What do we do all day? We look at the ancient buildings, swim in the local river, read books we haven't gotten to all year, and eat. Boy, do we eat.

I should explain that my father's main hobbies in life are (a) tennis and (b) cooking. In the summertime, I have always been his sous-chef, fixing a first course or chopping some shallots, but it's my pleasure (and JS's, and Will's, and Mom's) to sit back and just eat all the delicious food my father makes. Then wash the dishes afterward.

So in honor of Pop's years of culinary excellence, I'm including a menu of things he always makes for us on vacation.

And since you have to eat the next day, too, I've included a salad that we often have for lunch. It's very flexible and ingredients can be tossed or added as you wish. It's also a light dinner favorite.

Pop's All-Star Summer Revue

SOUPE AU PISTOU (PAGE 118)
&
RIB OF BEEF ON THE GRILL (PAGE 121)
&
POP'S FRIED ZUCCHINI (PAGE 122)
POP'S TOMATOES PROVENÇAL (PAGE 123)
&
POP'S CHOCOLATE SAUCE FOR ICE CREAM (PAGE 125)

Cool Lunch for a Hot Day

SALADE NIÇOISE COMPOSÉE (PAGE 126)
&
APRICOT-THYME CLAFOUTI (PAGE 130)

POP'S ALL-STAR SUMMER REVUE

Soupe au Pistou

As soon as I tell you these are all Pop's recipes, I immediately give one that's not. In fact, this is the recipe of our old next-door neighbor, Simone Vairon. Originally, it was the recipe of her mother, Madame Cogat. But every family in the south of France has a Soupe au Pistou recipe. It's practically the law. This one is very close to my heart—I have a picture of myself at two years old eating this very soup for lunch on the Vairons' terrace.

1 lb. fresh white shell beans, or the same amount of dried white beans, such as flageolet, cannellini, or white northern

1 large zucchini, cut into ½-inch dice

3 leeks, white parts only, cut in half and sliced ½-inch thick

½ lb. green beans, trimmed and cut into 1-inch lengths

3 carrots, peeled and cut into ½-inch-thick rounds

1 medium ripe tomato, cut in half

4 Yukon Gold potatoes, peeled and cut into ½-inch dice

1 tablespoon kosher salt

2 large cloves garlic, smashed and diced

1 large handful of basil leaves, torn up

⅓ cup olive oil

¼ lb. small elbow macaroni

Sea salt

Grated Gruyère or Swiss cheese and an old-fashioned French baguette, for serving

1. If you're using dried white beans, soak them in boiling water for an hour, until the beans are softened. If you're using fresh, obviously there's no soaking necessary—just add them with the rest of the veggies in step 2.
2. Put the first seven ingredients, through the potatoes, in the pressure cooker. (If you're using a standard soup pot, add the first six, through the tomato (the potato should be added toward the end of the cooking so it doesn't disintegrate). The pressure cooker should be filled with water up to the two-thirds safety line; the conventional soup pot should be filled with water until the vegetables are

submerged and covered by at least 2 inches. Add the tablespoon of kosher salt. Turn the heat on high and bring to a boil.

3. In the pressure cooker: Once at the boil, close the lid according to directions and bring to full pressure for 15 minutes, then allow the pressure cooker to release. In the conventional soup pot: once the soup begins to boil, turn down the heat and keep it at a very gentle simmer for an hour. Have the prepped potato at hand, and add it to the pot when there are 10 minutes left to go in the hour's cooking.

4. Once the cooking is finished, hunt about in the pot and locate the two halves of the tomato. Remove them from the pot and, after removing and tossing the skin, put the halves in a small bowl with the garlic, torn basil leaves, and olive oil. Mash everything around a bit with the back of a soup spoon to release the oils in the basil. Pour the lot back into the soup pot and stir to combine. Take a taste and see if you need some more kosher salt. At this point, bring the soup back to a gentle boil and add the macaroni. Cook for 10 minutes, until the macaroni is cooked through. Now season with some sea salt (the sea salt really sharpens the flavors of the veggies), and ladle into soup bowls. Serve with plenty of grated Gruyère and the baguette.

SPECIAL EQUIPMENT: *This soup is most easily made in a pressure cooker, but a regular soup pot will do.*
TIME: *1 hour in a pressure cooker, 2 with a standard soup pot*
FEEDS: *Oodles. OK, at least 10 in one sitting, but this soup is just as delicious for lunch the next day . . . or the day after that . . .*

Soupe Variants

I MENTIONED THAT every southern French family has its own recipe for Soupe au Pistou, and I've tasted a lot of them. The basic flavorings for the vegetables are the basil, garlic, oil, and tomato. Sometimes, they're cooked right in the soup, as they are here, but our friends Mag and Dominique serve their soup with a fresh tomato pureed with basil, olive oil, and garlic that you swirl into the soup before you top it with cheese. It's a lighter variant of the version on page 118.

BASIL (BASILIC)   +   GARLIC (AIL)   +   OLIVE OIL (HUILE D'OLIVE)   +   TOMATO (TOMATE)

Rib of Beef on the Grill

This is my absolute favorite way to have steak, though I can't make it at home because I don't have a grill. It is possible to make it in the broiler—placed on a bed of kosher salt and cracked pepper, and cooked for the same amount of time per side—but it doesn't match the grill's flavors and you must have an extremely well-ventilated kitchen.

1 whole rib of beef on the bone, about 2 inches thick (this is a specialty cut that the butcher at your market will have to prepare for you—definitely order it ahead of time)

A few tablespoons olive oil, for brushing

Kosher salt

Freshly ground black pepper

1. Preheat a grill to high. Prepare the meat by brushing it with a touch of oil, then salting it liberally and giving both sides an ample coating of pepper. Pops says no fewer than fifteen grindings per side.
2. Lower the meat onto the grill and sear quickly on both sides for about 2 minutes per side, then close the grill and cook the meat, turning once, until its internal temperature in the eye of the rib is 120°F (about 8 minutes per side). Check your thermometer vigilantly! At 120°F, meat is rare in the middle, but there will be plenty of medium-rare and even medium meat on the rib roast at this point.
3. Take the meat off the grill and let it rest on a platter for 10 minutes, then carve into ½-inch slices across the grain of the meat and serve.

SPECIAL EQUIPMENT: *A grill, long tongs, and, absolutely critical, an instant-read meat thermometer*
TIME: *About 25 minutes to cook the meat, plus time for your grill to come up to temperature*
FEEDS: *Surprisingly, considering the size of the rib, only 4*

= RIB OF BEEF =
BONE
2" THICK
RIBEYE

Pop's Fried Zucchini

This is what we always have on our first night of vacation. It might be the fresh country air, but it's always ambrosial.

4 large zucchini, peeled	Sea salt and black pepper, to taste
Salt	2 eggs
2 cups dried bread crumbs	2 tablespoons milk
⅓ cup finely chopped fresh flat-leaf parsley	Neutral vegetable oil (such as canola or safflower) for frying
½ cup grated Parmesan cheese	

1. Slice the zucchini into rounds about ¼-inch thick, slightly on the bias, so you get pretty oval shapes. Lightly salt the zukes.
2. On a dinner plate, combine the bread crumbs, parsley, and Parmesan cheese. Add some salt and pepper, and mix until uniformly distributed. In a soup plate, lightly beat together the two eggs with the milk. Line a platter or baking sheet with a length of waxed paper.
3. Next, line up the following in a row—zukes, eggs, bread crumbs, platter—then move down the line, dipping each piece of zucchini in egg, then coating it in bread crumbs before letting it take a breather on the waxed paper. If you need to layer the zucchini, simply separate the layers with more waxed paper. When you've coated all the slices, put the zucchini in the fridge to set up, at least an hour.
4. When you're ready to fry the zukes, heat ¼ inch of oil over medium-high heat until it's shimmering. If you feel up to it (and up to the cleanup that will be involved) you can do this in two skillets simultaneously. When the oil is hot, carefully lay the zucchini slices in the fat. Let them be for at least a minute—if you mess with them too quickly, the melting Parmesan can give you a sticky headache. Let them cook, moderating the heat to keep from burning them, about 3 minutes a side, or until a deep golden brown. You can keep them warm on a platter in a low oven while you finish up the others, or simply tent them with foil.
5. Sprinkle the finished product with some sea salt and eat right away.

TIME: *An hour or so to allow the breaded zucchini to set up in the refrigerator; about 40 minutes of working time*
FEEDS: *4 to 6 as a side dish*

Pop's Tomatoes Provençal

A simple summer treat.

4 medium-size ripe tomatoes

2 cloves garlic, minced

2 tablespoons chopped fresh basil

4 tablespoons olive oil

Salt and pepper

1. Preheat your oven to 375°F, or preheat your toaster oven to 350°F.
2. Cut the tops off the four tomatoes and discard. Give the tomatoes a squeeze into the garbage to get rid of some of the seeds. Set them on the counter to see if they'll sit upright. If they roll, cut a small sliver off the bottom to give them a comfortable place to sit.
3. Top each of the tomatoes with a bit of garlic, some chopped basil, and a tablespoon of olive oil. Sprinkle with salt and pepper, then transfer to a small gratin dish where they can fit snugly, or to the tray of your toaster oven (you can line it with foil first for ease of cleanup). Bake them for 20 minutes in the oven, or 15 minutes in the toaster oven, until they're a bit relaxed and juicy, but still standing on their own. Keep warm until you serve.

SPECIAL EQUIPMENT: *These can be made beautifully in the toaster oven, which has the added advantage of not heating up your entire kitchen.*
TIME: *Easily made while you shlurp a glass of rosé*
FEEDS: 4

Fromage!

a Cheese Play in Five Acts

ACT THREE: *The Old Stinkers*

SCENE: *Early Saturday morning, mid-July. Picturesque town square, filled with vegetable, fish, meat, and cheese stands—a French* marché. *In the middle of the square rests the moving-van-size cheese truck, with a long line of patient shoppers snaking from one end.* POP, J, *and* JS *stand on the line, carrying heavy bags of melons, zucchini, et cetera.* MOM *sits in a nearby café, drinking café au lait and reading the* International Herald Tribune.

J, *standing downwind of the truck, wrinkling her nose.* Whoo! This is a bit strong for 8 AM.

POP. When I die, I want to be laid out in the cheese truck. You won't be able to smell me for a month.

J. Thanks for that.

JS, *sniffing discerningly.* Which one smells like old shoes?

EPOISSES

POP, *cackling evilly.* That's the Reblochon. And it's on my list.

J, *resigned.* And what else?

POP. The Pont L'Évêque. And the Époisses.

JS. It's a good thing we eat outside.

(black out)

PONT L'EVEQUE

REBLOCHON

NOT ON LOVE ALONE

Pop's Chocolate Sauce for Ice Cream

This is a family tradition, adapted from Maida Heatter's Book of Great Chocolate Desserts. The original recipe calls for heavy cream, but Pop has always made it with crème fraîche in France. He once had to make it with yogurt, and it was delicious even so—a little zippy, actually!

Serve it over ice cream for the best chocolate sundae ever—the sauce firms up when it hits the cold ice cream, sliding off your spoon like molasses. Sometimes I ignore the ice cream and just eat the sauce.

½ cup crème fraîche or heavy cream

3 tablespoons unsalted butter

⅓ cup sugar

⅓ cup light brown sugar

pinch of salt

½ cup good-quality Dutch-process cocoa powder

In a small saucepan, melt the butter in the crème fraîche over medium-low heat, until the butter is melted and the mixture begins to boil. Add the sugars and stir until dissolved—a minute or two. Add the salt and cocoa powder, and combine with a whisk to prevent any lumps. When it's smooth and shiny, it's ready for the ice cream. You can keep it in the fridge or freeze it if you're not going to use it right away (just reheat it in a double boiler before serving).

SPECIAL EQUIPMENT: *If made ahead and you want to reheat, you'll need a double boiler, or 2 pots that work together as a double boiler.*
TIME: *5 minutes*
FEEDS: *6, copiously*

COOL LUNCH FOR A HOT DAY

ere's the thing: I love salad, but I love salad with things in it. Often, those things are shredded cheese and garlicky croutons. But Salade Niçoise satisfies my jones for variation, without necessarily adding impressive levels of fat and cholesterol. It's light, tasty, and all around, the perfect lunch salad.

Salade Niçoise Composée

I always like to lay out vegetables on top of a base of salad, so people can pick and choose their favorite elements and the heaviest stuff doesn't fall to the bottom of the salad bowl.

FOR THE SALAD:

1 red bell pepper

Head of lettuce, or a mix of lettuces, washed and dried

A handful of fresh basil

1 large (6-ounce) can fancy tuna packed in olive oil from Italy, such as Progresso, drained and flaked

¼ lb. string beans, prepped and blanched for 3 minutes in salted boiling water

2 hard-boiled eggs

¼ lb. new potatoes, boiled and sliced into bite-size pieces

1 large, ripe summer tomato, cut into wedges

FOR THE DRESSING:

2 tablespoons sherry vinegar

1 tablespoon Dijon mustard

⅓ cup olive oil

1 clove garlic, minced

1 teaspoon capers, drained and chopped

1 shallot, minced

Sea salt and pepper, to taste

NOT ON LOVE ALONE

1. Over an open burner on your stove, roast the red pepper on all sides until charred and black. (Use a pair of tongs to turn it, and before you begin move away any loose papers or other flammables in case of stray sparks. Don't worry— it's not as scary as it sounds.) Place the pepper in a zip-top bag and let it sit for 10 to 15 minutes. Take the pepper out of the bag and, rinsing it off as little as possible, peel and core it. Cut it into slivers.
2. Make the dressing: In a small bowl, combine the sherry vinegar and mustard until smooth, then slowly whisk in the olive oil. You should have a lovely emulsified vinaigrette. Add the garlic, capers, and shallot, and season to taste with salt and pepper.
3. Tear the lettuce into bite-size pieces; do the same with the basil. Toss to mix. Add half of the dressing—just enough to very lightly coat the leaves.
4. To serve, heap the lettuce and the basil leaves in the center of a large platter. Put the tuna on top, then arrange the veggies and egg wedges around the edge in groups so it looks like something out of a painting. Drizzle with some extra dressing. Then say in French, "*Voilà!*"

SPECIAL EQUIPMENT: *Nothing more complicated than a can opener and a zip-top bag*
TIME: *30 minutes assembling the ingredients*
FEEDS: *6, pretty easily*

Summer Salad

For me, lettuce does not define a salad. Particularly in the summer, when so many tasty vegetables are at their peak, I like to use them as the base, instead.

One of the most well known summer salads is the *Caprese*: basil, tomato, and mozzarella. When the tomatoes are ripe, there's nothing better, but I like to play around with it, sometimes adding slices of avocado, or changing the components to grape tomatoes, feta, and mint.

Another vegetable I like to use as a salad base is zucchini, as in my suggestion for zukes, almonds, and Parmesan, an idea I've borrowed from a New York restaurant called the Red Cat. You can sauté the zucchini with a bit of olive oil and lemon juice, and serve it at room temperature, tossed with the nuts and cheese.

If you must have lettuce, tweak the ratio and instead of having it be the focus of the salad, treat it as one of many ingredients. That's how I like my salad of avocado, Boston lettuce, and peas.

As for dressings, in the summer, lighter is better. A mixture of lemon juice and hazelnut oil, or a little sweet balsamic vinegar whisked with olive oil is all you need. Sometimes, I rub the inside of a salad bowl with a cut clove of garlic, then at the last second toss lettuce with a few dribbles of excellent olive oil. Of course, sea salt and freshly ground pepper are summer salad absolutes!

Three Summer Salads:

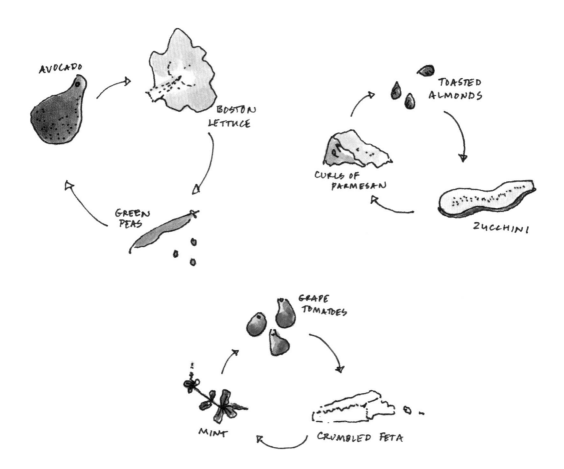

AVOCADO

BOSTON
LETTUCE

GREEN
PEAS

TOASTED
ALMONDS

CURLS OF
PARMESAN

ZUCCHINI

GRAPE
TOMATOES

MINT

CRUMBLED FETA

Apricot-Thyme Clafouti

*I*t's a no-brainer that fruit desserts are best in season, but you can make this fruit-studded custard with high-quality canned apricots in light syrup any time of year. Just drain the apricots before you use them and reduce the sugar by one tablespoon. I prefer cooked apricots to raw ones, anyway. I think that, cooked, they lose a certain mealiness that always competes with their wonderful flavor.

2 tablespoons butter, plus extra for greasing the baking dish

4 tablespoons sugar, plus ½ cup

A few sprigs of fresh thyme

3 cups pitted and halved apricots

4 large eggs

1 cup milk

½ vanilla bean, halved lengthwise

½ cup all-purpose flour

pinch of salt

1. Grease a pie pan or ceramic baking dish and set aside.
2. Place a nonstick skillet (if you've got one) over high heat for a minute. Turn down the heat to medium-high and melt the butter. When the foam subsides, add the 4 tablespoons of sugar, the thyme, and the apricots. Let them sit there for a minute. Then carefully stir them with a spoon, or do the fancy chef trick of flipping the contents of your pan over with the flick of your wrist. Be careful—you don't want the apricots to fall apart. Depending on their ripeness, you'll be done after 3 to 5 minutes—the apricots should be a little softened and golden but not mushy. Set aside to cool.
3. Make the custard: In a bowl, beat together the eggs and remaining ½ cup of sugar with a whisk until frothy—a minute or so. Scrape the innards of the vanilla bean into the milk (you can toss the cleaned pod into your sugar bowl if you'd like to have vanilla sugar around). Add the milk to the egg mixture and mix until combined. Add the flour and salt—gradually, so it doesn't lump up too badly; give it a good whisk. Preheat oven to 375°F

4. In the greased pie pan or ceramic baking dish, strew the apricots and thyme in an even layer. Then pour the custard over them. Pop it into the oven—it'll take 25 to 35 minutes and will be done when it has puffed up a bit and is golden brown. Serve at room temperature. Yum!

SPECIAL EQUIPMENT: *A nonstick skillet and an ovenproof baking dish*
TIME: *1 hour*
FEEDS: *6 people who really like dessert*

❤ FRUIT ❤ HERBS ❤

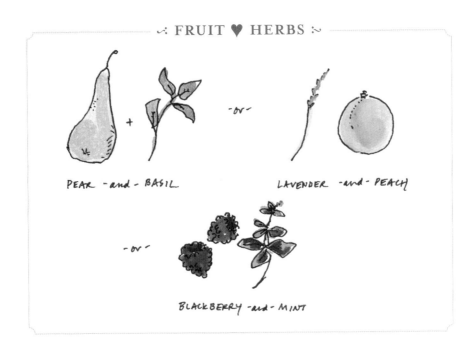

PEAR -and- BASIL

-or-

LAVENDER -and- PEACH

-or-

BLACKBERRY -and- MINT

AUGUST

On Our Best (or Worst) Behavior

On Our Best (or Worst) Behavior

There comes a time in every young couple's life where it will be necessary to impress someone, and it might happen at home. These days, it's probably not your boss, but most likely your in-laws, or worse, your own parents. You know: they're in town, you've already gone out (on their dime, of course) once or twice, and you're starting to feel guilty about a whole host of things . . . the cost of the wedding . . . how you haven't used the set of knives they gave you for your engagement present . . . the list is endless. So to make it up to them, you decide to make dinner at home. Thus, my Meet the Parents menu.

This is the right menu in so many ways: it's elegant but not ambitious in terms of flavor; it uses the best the summer has to offer; and it's very doable ahead of time with some strategic reheating.

Plus, when your duty is done, you get to cheer yourself up by having a boozy cocktail party for your friends, but with something more elegant than a case of Coors Light and bowls of nacho chips. Make a few simple snacks, like the ones I've included later in this chapter, and people will think you're some kind of entertaining wunderkind. And if you have access to a little outdoor space (my playground is my roof, accessed via the fire escape—no, not legal), with a nice view of the summer sunset, a late-August Saturday-night cocktail party will flood your guests with bonhomie (which means when they come over next time they might bring you a bottle of Champagne or something).

Meet the Parents

TOMATO BRUSCHETTA (PAGE 136)

&

ROASTED CHICKEN WITH WATERCRESS (PAGE 138)

&

CORN GRIDDLE CAKES (PAGE 141)

&

ICE CREAM WITH CARAMEL AND TOASTED ALMONDS (PAGE 144)

Summer Cocktail Party

QUAIL EGGS WITH CELERY SALT (PAGE 145)
RUBBED TOAST (PAGE 146)
FRIED SQUASH BLOSSOMS (PAGE 147)
FENNEL AND TAPENADE ON TOAST (PAGE 148)
RADISHES WITH BUTTER AND SALT (PAGE 149)
TOMATOES STUFFED WITH FETA AND CHIVES (PAGE 150)

&

BELLINIS (PAGE 151)
PINEAPPLE VODKA TONICS (PAGE 154)

MEET THE PARENTS

This is a recipe that is open to interpretation and thus the amounts are a little fluid. Just play around with it—you don't want it to be dry, but tomato soup is not the goal!

2 cloves garlic

1 tablespoon Dijon mustard

3 tablespoons sherry vinegar

¼ cup good olive oil—more as needed

Salt and pepper, to taste

3 to 4 large, very ripe tomatoes

A handful of basil leaves

6 slices of good country bread, preferably from yesterday

1. Mince 1 garlic clove. Then throw it into a large bowl—big enough to hold all the tomatoes—along with the mustard and vinegar, and mix with a fork until combined. Then add the olive oil in a slow, steady stream, mixing all the while. Do this until you have a vinaigrette that's not too vinegary, since the massive amount of garlic will take care of that. Add salt and pepper, to taste.
2. Core and dice the tomatoes into bite-size chunks. Stick 'em in the large bowl and tear up a bunch of basil—as much as you want. Throw in the basil with the tomatoes. Let the whole thing sit and stew at room temperature for at least 30 minutes.
3. Toast the bread in your toaster (or conventional) oven until quite toasty, but not so dark that you have to scrape it into the trash. Cut the other garlic clove in half and rub the cut sides on the slices of toast. Rub it like you mean it! You can do all of this several hours ahead.

NOT ON LOVE ALONE

4. Put a slice of toast in the bottom of a shallow soup bowl and ladle a generous helping of tomato on top, making sure to get lots of the lovely vinaigrette and tomato juices. Serve it up.

TIME: *10 to 15 minutes of working time, plus time to let the tomatoes marinate*
FEEDS: *6 as a first course*

⤋ GETTING RID OF GARLIC SMELLS ∿

*T*HEY SELL FANCY bars of "soap" at gourmet shops to help you get rid of garlicky hands, but all you have to do is this: wash your hands under hot water with regular soap, all the while rubbing your fingertips on a stainless-steel utensil. It works.

Roasted Chicken with Watercress

A lovely combination of chicken and greens. It might sound like a bad idea to roast a chicken in August, but I love the tomato-corn-chicken triumvirate that's best in high summer. What I do is roast the chicken earlier in the day, before the guests come, and serve it at room temperature, with the sauce just lightly reheated in a small pan on top of the stove. That way our tragically small air conditioner has had time to win the battle against our little furnace . . . I mean, oven.

A very nice chicken, preferably free-range, 3 to 4 pounds

Kosher salt and pepper

1 onion, unpeeled and split in half

½ lemon

2 or 3 strips bacon

½ to ¾ cup water or white wine

A bunch of watercress, washed and dried

1. Preheat the oven to 425°F.
2. Rinse the ol' bird and pat her dry. Put her on a rack in the middle of a snug roasting pan. Salt and pepper the cavity, then put the neck, gizzard, and heart inside; discard the liver.
3. Wedge inside half of the onion and the lemon half. Drape the bacon over the breasts and the tops of the drumsticks. Salt and pepper the outside. Throw the other half of the onion in the bottom of the roasting pan, along with ¼ cup of water.
4. Get the bird in the oven. Wait! Don't walk away . . . you have work to do. Every 15 minutes you have to baste the bird—the bacon helps you, because it sort of bastes the chicken itself. But don't forget, or you'll be sorry!
5. A 3- to 4-pound bird will probably take 1½ hours to cook, but sometimes things go slower or faster, so the best way to check is to periodically stick a meat thermometer in at the junction of breast and thigh, taking the bird out when you hit 170°F. Just be careful not to have the tip of the thermometer resting on the bone, or you'll have an overly high temperature reading. If, toward the last half-hour of the cooking time, the bacon is looking petrified, take it off and let the bird brown beautifully.
6. Take the bird out of the oven. Lift it out of the roasting pan, draining the juices back into the pan, and put it on a platter tented with tinfoil for as long as you like. Personally, I like my roast chicken lukewarm. Meanwhile . . .

7. Remove the roasting rack from the pan and place it on the stove over medium-high heat. Scrape up all the good bits from the bottom of the pan. You can scoop out the onion and skim off some of the excess fat now. Add some water or wine—between ½ and ¾ cup—and let bubble over and cook down a bit—about 5 minutes. Transfer the sauce to a serving dish.

8. Carve the chicken, arranging it on a platter: take off the legs and thighs as one, then slice each pair through the joint to separate them. Slice off the wings, close to their joint, then make a long incision down the center back of the breast, using a knife and your fingers to lift one side of the breast, then the other, entirely off the bone. Slice crosswise into thick strips, letting each serving retain its burnished, crispy skin.

9. Toss the watercress with a squeeze of the lemon from the cavity of the chicken and a tablespoon or two of the pan drippings. Place it on the platter with the chicken, and serve the remaining sauce on the side.

SPECIAL EQUIPMENT: *A roasting rack, and a roasting pan that can go from your oven to the top of the stove (glass and ceramic are out)*
TIME: *2 hours*
FEEDS: *4 to 6, depending on the crowd*

↶ THE GREAT CHICKEN DEBATE ↷

To Truss or Not to Truss

*T*HERE ARE RAGING debates (really!) about whether it's better to truss the chicken, have the chicken let it all hang out, or let it all hang out within the confines of a roasting rack (my choice). There are valid arguments for each side. My advice? Perform some experiments and decide which you like the best.

 vs

A Note on Salt

ONCE, I HAD the opportunity to hear Barbara Kafka, a wonderful chef and cookbook author, lecture on salt. I confess that before then I had not given salt the amount of time and energy it deserves. But after Barbara Kafka's talk, I was galvanized. No more would I use standard table salt, which has (I realized, now that it had been pointed out to me) a distinctively bitter iodine flavor. No, instead I would rely on the delicate salinity of kosher salt in my everyday cooking. I'd splurge on astoundingly expensive French sea salt from the Île de Ré for my salads. But it *does* make a difference. Try it and see.

Corn Griddle Cakes

So . . . yeah, you could just boil up some corn (hint: with sugar, not salt, in the water) and eat it the way God intended—that is, with salt, pepper, and butter. But if you're feeling crazy (and stressing to impress), make these. This is a recipe of my father's. The corn cakes can be made ahead and rewarmed in the oven after the chicken comes out, or just served at room temperature.

4 ears corn, husks and silk removed

1 egg, lightly beaten

¼ cup all-purpose flour

¼ cup grated Parmesan cheese

Some fresh chives, snipped

Kosher salt and pepper

1 tablespoon unsalted butter

1. Cut the corn off the cobs (see Cutting Corn from the Cob, page 142). Put the kernels in a large bowl; then, using a box grater, grate the remaining cobs over the same large bowl to get the juice and any leftover corn kernels your knife might have missed. It should end up being a mélange of whole kernels, half kernels, and milky corn liquid. Discard cobs. Stir in the egg, flour, cheese, and chives, and season with salt and pepper. The batter will be quite thick but should be uniformly mixed.
2. Melt the butter over medium heat in a nonstick skillet. Spoon the batter in ¼-cup doses into the hot pan. Leave them be for a few minutes, or the Parmesan might make the corn cakes adhere to the bottom of the pan. Cook them until golden brown on one side, then flip and brown the other side, about 8 minutes total. Drain on paper towels.

SPECIAL EQUIPMENT: *A nonstick pan is essential here.*
TIME: *15 to 20 minutes active time*
FEEDS: *6*

⌣ CUTTING CORN FROM THE COB ⌣

A GOOD TRICK is to surround the base of each cob with a kitchen towel as you cut down (and away from yourself). Corn loves to fly, so the kitchen towel catches any escapees.

Green-market Eating

OR ME, THE best part about cooking in the summertime is the Union Square Greenmarket's extravaganza of fruits and vegetables. In the spring or fall I often go to the market myself mid-morning, but in the summer I rouse JS with the promise of a real breakfast if he comes with me to the green market and carries the bags. (We also have a little collapsible shopping cart that is very desirable for this, the proof being that several old ladies have come up to us and complimented us upon it.)

The Union Square Greenmarket is just the hub of dozens of farmers' markets that dot the city from day to day. As the main one, it's open four days a week, with the largest markets on Friday and Saturday. It's always a bit hard for me to control myself in the market during the summer. I have to be very strict about the amount of money I'm willing to spend, or else I'll come home with a large selection of adorable, strange, and somewhat pricey rare fruits and vegetables. My heirloom-tomato budget, alone . . .

Farmers' market shopping is a valuable way to educate yourself about what fruit and vegetables are really supposed to smell, feel, look, and taste like. If you don't know where to find a farmers' market near you, try the USDA's Web site at www.ams.usda.gov. You can also check local magazines and newspapers for locations.

Ice Cream with Caramel and Toasted Almonds

There's no better, or easier, dessert in the summer than ice cream, since somebody else has made it for you. I do like to fuss about with toppings, however. Here's a good one.

1 handful raw almonds

1 cup sugar

¼ cup water

½ cup or more heavy cream

Squeeze of lemon juice

1 tablespoon unsalted butter

Store-bought vanilla ice cream

1. Toast the almonds at 350°F in your toaster oven (which someone is sure to have given you as a wedding present). When they're done—they should be lightly golden—give 'em a very rough chop. Set aside.
2. Put the sugar in a small, heavy-bottomed saucepan. Carefully pour ¼ cup of water on top. Run your finger though the sugar to make sure it's all been moistened. Turn the heat on to medium.
3. Don't touch the pan! Watch the sugar until it has all dissolved. *Then* you can give it a very gentle swirl. Cook it, swirling once or twice, until it is a nice dark amber color, 8 to 10 minutes. Be careful as you get to the end of the cooking time, as burnt sugar is not a joy to clean.
4. Off the heat, pour in the heavy cream and stir like you mean it. It'll boil furiously and look like a mistake for a few moments, but don't worry. When it's smooth, you can add a little more heavy cream to taste if the caramel is too strong for you. Add the lemon juice and the butter, and stir until the butter is melted. The caramel will thicken as it cools. Leave it on the counter until you need it, but it should be refrigerated overnight (and can stay in there for weeks for future ice cream adornments).
5. At dessert time, scoop out some vanilla ice cream and top with a spoonful or two (or three) of caramel and a sprinkle of chopped almonds. You could also add some raspberries if you'd like.

TIME: *10 minutes to make the sauce and toast the almonds*
FEEDS: *This recipe makes about 1 cup of sauce.*

NOT ON LOVE ALONE

SUMMER COCKTAIL PARTY

You've just been on your best behavior. . . now for your worst. The tidbits and hors d'oeuvres here are very simple, and can be scattered around the party on platters so guests can feed themselves. This is a true cocktail party, so there's not enough food here to sustain hours of drinking and talking—if guests stay too late, order a pizza. But there's plenty of food for fifteen people in a two- to three-hour window.

Quail Eggs with Celery Salt

30 quail eggs
Celery salt

Sea salt

At my butcher shop, quail eggs come in flats of thirty. They're adorable, speckled things, and when you crack them, the inside of the shell is a delicate celadon green. Their flavor is chicken-eggy, but more delicate and a bit sweeter. All you need to do is set them in barely boiling water for 5 minutes, run them under the cold tap to cool them, and serve them in a bowl with a dish of sea salt and a dish of celery salt alongside. Sometimes I partially peel a few to encourage eaters, but at a recent party (and I think this tells you something about the sort of people JS and I spend time with) people were breaking the quail eggshells on their foreheads. Of course, that was *after* the keg stands . . .

Rubbed Toast

It's very hard to say just how much bread you might want here, because it depends on the size of the loaf. What I can tell you is that you want to cut it into bite-size wedges, each about the size of a tortilla chip, before you serve it; each wedge counts as a serving. Your goal here is about 40 servings.

Several ½-inch slices country bread

2 cloves garlic, halved

2 very ripe tomatoes

Olive oil

¼ lb. prosciutto, sliced very thin

10 anchovies cured in oil

Sea salt

1. Using your toaster, or a grill pan with ridges, toast or grill the bread until it's very dark but not burned. Immediately rub one side of the toast with a half clove of garlic.
2. Cut the tomatoes in half and rub the cut sides against the toast, really soaking the bread with the juices. Use each half-tomato until it's given all it can give, juice-wise, then move on to the next. Drizzle each slice with a hint of olive oil. Cut the toast into wedges. Sprinkle about twenty with sea salt. Lay a thin slice of prosciutto on ten others, giving it an attractive ripple when you cover the bread. Finally, garnish ten others with an anchovy curled up loosely in the center. Arrange the toasts casually on a platter and put it out for your guests to enjoy.

TIME: *15 minutes*

FEEDS: *This recipe makes 40 portions.*

NOT ON LOVE ALONE

Fried Squash Blossoms

I have a thing for these, but whether it's the idea of eating a blossom, or the whole fried batter—salt angle, I don't know. You shouldn't make these years ahead of time, but they drain very easily on a cookie rack on top of some paper towel, and are just as good at room temperature as they are warm. Just remember to salt them liberally.

20 zucchini or squash blossoms

Olive oil, for frying

1⅓ cup all-purpose flour

1 cup seltzer water

Sea salt

1. Carefully rinse the blossoms and dry them on paper towels or a clean kitchen towel. They need to be as dry as you can get them.
2. Fill a large skillet ¼ inch up the side with olive oil, and turn the heat to medium. Roll out some paper towel and put a cookie rack over it.
3. While the oil's heating, make the batter, which is essentially paste: Sift the flour into a medium-size bowl, then, stirring constantly with a whisk, add the seltzer in a slow, steady stream until the batter has the consistency of sour cream or pancake batter.
4. Using a deft, light touch, hold each blossom by its stem end and give the flower a quick swirl in the batter. (It's a good idea to have the batter bowl right next to the stove.) Lay the flower in the hot oil (it might pop a bit, so be prepared to stand back). Continue with the other blossoms, stopping when the pan is full but each blossom has room to breathe. Turn the blossoms over with tongs as they become golden, then fish the finished blossoms out of the oil with the strainer or slotted spoon. Sprinkle them with salt. Let them rest on the cookie rack. Keep them at room temperature until you need them. These will go quickly.

SPECIAL EQUIPMENT: *A bamboo-handled strainer, the sort you can find at Chinese cooking-supply stores, is very useful here, but your average slotted spoon will do in a pinch.*
TIME: *30 minutes*
FEEDS: *This recipe makes 20 blossoms.*

Fennel and Tapenade on Toast

This was an hors d'oeuvre I started making after eating something similar at 'ino, a paninoteca on Bedford Street, a few blocks from our apartment. This little cubbyhole of a restaurant serves grilled panini, but also has a selection of excellent (and reasonably priced) bruschettas. Sometimes in a pinch before a dinner party, I send JS down there to get a plate full of them, which I then cut in half for hors d'oeuvres. Unconventional takeout, to be sure, but nobody complains!

A baguette, sliced very thinly on the bias, at least 25 slices

1 large, squat bulb of fennel, stalks and bottom trimmed

Juice of ½ lemon

3 tablespoons good olive oil

Sea salt and pepper

¼ cup tapenade (French black-olive spread) purchased at a gourmet shop, or ¼ cup finely chopped cured black Provençal olives

1. Preheat your oven to 250°F. Alternatively, use your toaster oven on the lowest setting. Lay the baguette slices out in a single layer on a cookie sheet and pop them in the oven. Let them toast for 30 minutes, until they're crispy like a cracker and slightly blond about the edges.
2. Meanwhile, cut the fennel bulb in half and slice it as thinly as you can on a mandoline. If the fennel is really fat and squat, you might have to cut it to quarters to achieve the ease of mandolining. You should have about 3 cups of tissue-thin fennel. Move the shaved fennel to a bowl and toss it with the lemon juice, olive oil, a pinch of sea salt, and some pepper. Set aside for 15 minutes to allow the flavors to commingle.
3. When the toasts have come out of the oven, let them cool, then top them with a tablespoon of the fennel and a small dab of the tapenade. Arrange them on a platter and serve.

SPECIAL EQUIPMENT: *A mandoline, which can be purchased in plastic for less than $20 and is invaluable for slicing fennel, potatoes, or apples paper thin*
TIME: *30 minutes*
FEEDS: *This makes about 25 toasts.*

NOT ON LOVE ALONE

Radishes with Butter and Salt

2 bunches of radishes
(you want about 35 radishes)

Slab of very good French butter, a bit soft

Small pile of sea salt

This is beyond easy and very tasty, the heat of the radishes tempered by the creaminess of the butter and made more flavorful by the sea salt. Some people (by which I mean, healthy people) like to dip their radishes in ice water and then into the salt, bypassing the butter. That produces a sharper, spicier flavor. All you need to do is clean and trim the radishes, and display them prettily alongside the butter and the salt on a platter. I always include a small knife or two to aid with the butter, though if it's very soft the radish can do all the work itself.

Tomatoes Stuffed with Feta and Chives

The most amazing thing about cocktail parties is that the thing that takes the longest to make is always the first to disappear down people's throats.

1 cup feta cheese, crumbled (goat's-milk feta is best)

¼ cup good olive oil

¼ cup snipped fresh chives

Freshly ground pepper

Kosher salt, to taste

1 pint cherry tomatoes

Fresh chive tips for decoration

1. First, make the filling: In a small bowl or a zip-top bag, combine the crumbled feta, the olive oil, and the snipped chives, along with a hearty helping of pepper. Taste for salt before you add any—feta can pack a pretty salty punch. Combine and set aside at room temperature.
2. Prep the tomatoes: Cut the tops off and discard them. Using a melon baller or teaspoon, hollow out the tomatoes, tossing the seeds. Then, slice a minuscule layer off the bottom of the cherry tomatoes, barely more than the skin, just enough to give the tomato a less precarious perch. Line them up on a plate.
3. Fill the suckers: Take a teaspoon and fill each tomato so there's a nice little mound above the rim. Top with a longer chive tip for that Martha Stewart touch. Repeat, repeat, repeat.

SPECIAL EQUIPMENT: *Get ready . . . I'm going to tell you to use a melon baller. Don't have one? For shame! Actually, neither do I. You can use a small teaspoon.*
TIME: *45 minutes*
FEEDS: *This recipe makes about 25 stuffed tomatoes.*

Bellinis

Famously invented at Harry's Bar in Venice, a Bellini is a sweet-tart summertime drink that makes the best use of peaches this side of peach pie. You can make your own puree, as I do here, or you can be lazy and buy peach nectar, tarted up with some lemon juice.

½ lb. very ripe white peaches

Juice of ½ lemon

¼ cup water

A few teaspoons of sugar, to taste

Raspberries

A bottle of Prosecco (Italian sparkling wine) (See Champagne and Other Bubblies on page 42)

1. Loosen the peach skins by submerging the peaches in boiling water for 30 seconds, then running them under cold water. Peel the peaches (the skin should slip off easily), pit them, and cut them into hunks. Cover them with the lemon juice and water. Let them sit about 15 minutes.
2. Slide the peaches into the blender, and give them a whiz. Taste for sugar—it shouldn't be too tart, but we're not making piña coladas here. Elegantly fruity should be the goal. Pour the puree into a pitcher and refrigerate it.
3. To serve, drop a raspberry into the bottom of a champagne flute, then add a dollop of the peach puree. Fill the rest of the glass with Prosecco.

SPECIAL EQUIPMENT: *A blender*
TIME: *20 minutes*
QUENCHES: *Face it, if you have friends like ours, you need to double this recipe. Makes about 8 Bellinis.*

Quick Notes on Summertime Entertaining

$\mathcal{T}$HE BEST PART of summer entertaining is how easily it falls into your lap. There are cheap flowers everywhere, and everything that's delicious seems to be in season. You just have to collect it and present it to your guests.

- Watch the weather. If it's going to be ninety-five degrees, don't start the party at 6:00 PM. Part of the joy of a summer weekend is how late things can begin because of the late sunsets. Don't broil your guests but plan ahead and invite them for when things might be a little bit cooler.

- On that note, keep an ample supply of nonalcoholic drinks on hand, particularly sparkling water with some lemon. Dehydration is not pretty. Also, get an extra bag of ice.

- Alcohol, on the other hand, should be carefully considered. I would stick with a special drink (like the two I've given here), plus some white wine and bottled beer on ice. If you're doing this inside, and you have an all-white decorating scheme, skip red wine entirely.

For decoration, why not group about the cheapest of the farmers' market blooms—wildflowers—in vases of different heights? Choose flowers that are either all the same color, or variants in the same color family. It looks very pretty and expensive, even if it's not. You could also nix the buds and decorate with summer fruits—bowls of small plums and platters of grapes and late summer figs are particularly pretty.

Pineapple Vodka Tonics

My cousin Patty made these when she hosted our engagement party. *They're delicious, refreshing, and have the fatal flaw of not tasting like they're going to get you drunk. In other words, the perfect drink if you want a happening cocktail party.*

1 pineapple	Tonic water
A 750-ml bottle of decent vodka. Spring for Absolut or something like it.	Fresh mint sprigs for garnish

1. Peel the pineapple: Cut the crown and the base off the pineapple, then, using your paring (or boning) knife, slice off the skin and discard. Quarter the fruit with a chef's knife, then slice straight down at the right angle of each quarter, cutting away the core (discard). Slice three of the four quarters of remaining pineapple into 1-inch chunks; slice the last quarter into thin slices for presentation, and wrap these last slices in plastic wrap until you need them.
2. Place the pineapple chunks in a large pitcher with a tight-fitting lid, or a large jar with a lid (or several large jars). Decant the vodka over the fruit, close the lid tightly, and let steep in a cool place (or the fridge) for at least a day (two days is better).
3. To serve, pour 1 part pineapple vodka to 2 parts tonic water over ice, and add a mint sprig and a slice of pineapple.

TIME: *At least a day for the vodka to infuse; actual time of cocktail making, negligible*
QUENCHES: *Quite a few, I hope! About 15.*

NOT ON LOVE ALONE

September

Italian-Indian Summer

Italian-Indian Summer

T HE END OF September will be the last gasp of the tomato . . . eat 'em up now, for too soon we'll have only those horrible pinkish things shipped in from unspecified South American countries to choose from.

Late-summer tomatoes are a little softer, so ripe they're in danger of going over the edge. Meanwhile, the zucchinis are still going strong, vessels for any flavor you want to add to them—garlic, onions, salt, lemon. And the peaches are on their last legs, so do yourself a favor and eat one more peach dessert before next August.

The centerpiece of The Last Gasp menu is tomato risotto, which, though one of my favorite dishes, is not the only way to use up juicy, overripe late summer tomatoes. You can do a similar dish with orzo; or cut up tomatoes, toss them with some garlic, fresh basil, and olive oil, and—*tada!*—you have a raw sauce for hot pasta. Another option is a *panzanella*, a salad made from tomatoes, fresh basil, and day-old bread, terrific alongside grilled steak.

Speaking of basil, one thing that regularly confounds me is the size of a bunch of basil these days. At farmers' markets and supermarkets alike, you don't get the little nosegay of basil you need for a few strategic snips onto a tomato salad, but instead you get what I think of, for lack of a better description, as a basil *tree*. So after you've used a dainty leaf or two on your salad, you need only make three hundred more before the basil is used up. That's where basil-accented pastas come in handy. Whether it's just the leaves or a full-on pesto, pasta helps solve the surplus basil problem beautifully.

The Last Gasp Menu

STUFFED ZUCCHINI WITH GOAT CHEESE (PAGE 158)

&

TOMATO RISOTTO (PAGE 160)

&

FAST PEACH TART (PAGE 162)

Three Basil Pastas

FUSILLI WITH ZUCCHINI, GARLIC, AND BASIL (PAGE 164)

&

FARFALLE WITH RICOTTA, LEMON, BASIL, AND PEAS (PAGE 165)

&

SPAGHETTI PESTO WITH CROUTONS (PAGE 166)

THE LAST GASP

Stuffed Zucchini with Goat Cheese

In France, they have these perfect little round courgettes that are excellent for stuffing. Here, just get the smallest, cutest zukes you can find. If you go for a regular-size squash, I personally think half a zucchini is enough, but eat up a whole one if you prefer (just double the recipe).

4 small (no less than 4 inches long) or 2 medium-size zucchini

2 tablespoons olive oil

2 medium onions, sliced very thin into half-moons

½ cup white wine

1 cake of the freshest goat cheese you can find (about ½ cup), crumbled

¼ cup chopped basil

2 tablespoons chopped mint

Kosher salt and pepper

1 tablespoon plain dried bread crumbs

1. Set up a steamer that can fit all of the whole zucchini at one time. Fill the bottom of the pot with at least 4 inches of water, cover, and bring to a boil. In the meantime, prep the zukes: If you're using the little squashes that look like mini pumpkins, cut the tops off, reserve, and then attack the innards of the zucchini with a teaspoon, hollowing the whole thing out without doing damage to the structural integrity of the vegetable. Keep the zucchini innards in a pile on your cutting board for later. For the smaller version of conventional zucchini, slice off the top quarter lengthwise and keep that as a lid; hollow out the rest. Normal-size zucchini should be cut in half lengthwise, and both sides hollowed out. Salt the cavities of your zucchini.
2. Get the suckers into the steamer, cut side down, including the caps. Close the lid, and let the zukes steam until the flesh can be comfortably pierced with the tip of a paring knife but they don't show any signs of collapse, about 5 minutes. They should still be the brightest green. Take them out of the steamer and set aside.

3. Now for the filling: finely chop the reserved zucchini innards. Then, heat the olive oil in a large skillet over high heat until it shimmers. Add the sliced onion, season with salt, and give it a healthy sauté for 8 to 10 minutes. You want the onion to become a rich, tawny caramel color. At this point, add the chopped zucchini, another pinch of salt, and a generous amount of pepper, and stir to combine. Add the white wine, turn the heat down to medium-low, and let the wine boil off completely, about 4 to 6 minutes. Pour the contents of the pan into a large mixing bowl and set aside to cool.
4. Preheat the oven to 450°F.
5. When the filling is just a bit warm, fold in the crumbled goat cheese and the herbs. Test for seasoning—beware of adding too much salt, as the goat cheese can be quite salty. Arrange the zuke shells in a baking dish, fill each cavity generously, then sprinkle the tops with a light dusting of dried bread crumbs. Add another drizzle of olive oil. Perch the caps on top, then carefully slide them into the oven. Bake for 12 to 15 minutes, or until the bread crumbs have browned and the cheese is bubbling away. Serve hot.

SPECIAL EQUIPMENT: *An ovenproof ceramic baking dish; a colander or perforated insert for a pot for steaming*
TIME: *About 1 hour, including baking time*
FEEDS: *4*

Tomato Risotto

Risotto is hands-on all the way—the constant stirring keeps the rice from sticking and builds up the lovely starches that make it so creamy. There are some wonderful herbs in this risotto, but the most distinctive is the marjoram, which I suggest making the extra effort to find fresh. Just a small pinch will perfume the whole dish.

4 medium, very ripe tomatoes

5 cups chicken stock

3 tablespoons unsalted butter

1 tablespoon olive oil

½ small onion, chopped fine

1 very small clove garlic, minced

Sea salt and freshly ground black pepper

2 cups Arborio rice

Heaping ½ cup freshly grated Parmesan cheese

½ cup chopped fresh herbs, including basil, marjoram, and flat-leaf parsley

Shaved Parmesan cheese and torn basil leaves, for garnish

1. Peel the tomatoes: bring a pot of water to a boil. Drop the tomatoes in, one by one, for about 30 seconds. Run these under cold water, cut an X-shaped incision into the skin, and pull the skin off. Then, seed and dice them.
2. Pour the stock into a pot and heat to the simmer.
3. In a medium-size heavy-bottomed saucepan, melt 2 tablespoons of the butter with the 1 tablespoon of olive oil. When the foam subsides, add the onion and garlic, and cook over medium heat until translucent, a few minutes. Add the tomatoes, a pinch of salt and grinding of pepper, give a stir, and turn the heat down to low. Cook, stirring occasionally, for 10 minutes—you want the tomatoes to break down, but not completely.
4. Add the Arborio rice to the tomato mixture and stir to coat with a wooden spoon. Turn the heat up to medium, or even medium-high—risotto needs a lively flame and should never be soupy. Starting with ½ cup and then additional ¼ cups, add the simmering broth to the rice, stirring all the while. Once the liquid has evaporated, you can add some more. After about 15 minutes taste a few grains. You don't want mushy rice; it should still be slightly firm (but not crunchy!).

Not on Love Alone

5. When you estimate you have about 5 minutes left to go, add the remaining table-spoon of butter, the Parmesan cheese, and the chopped herbs. Turn down the heat to low and continue adding the stock. You should now have that wonderful creamy risotto consistency, with the rice tinted pink from the tomatoes. Taste for salt and adjust as necessary. Garnish with shaved Parmesan cheese and torn basil leaves, and serve.

TIME: *35 minutes*
FEEDS: *4, generously*

= BEEFSTEAK

= GRAPE TOMATOES

= HEIRLOOMS

= SUPERMARKET IN JANUARY

Fast Peach Tart

The hardest part of this tart is peeling the peaches, which you can do the same way you peel tomatoes, in boiling water—leave them in for a full minute. So it ain't very hard at all, actually . . .

A sheet of prepared puff pastry from the freezer section, defrosted

3 tablespoons butter

6 ripe peaches

4 tablespoons sugar

1. Preheat the oven to 425°F.
2. Make sure the puff pastry is completely thawed. Unfold the sheet onto a nonstick cookie sheet that's been greased with a tiny bit of butter. If you don't have a nonstick sheet, use a cookie sheet lined with parchment paper that's been greased with a bit of butter. Prick the center of the puff pastry with a fork a few times. Stick it in the fridge.
3. Microwave the butter so it melts (or melt it in a small pan on the stove).
4. Slice the peaches by cutting the fruit in half to stone it, then slicing each half into ¼-inch-thick half-moons rather than into wedges, as you might for a pie—the uniform thickness is important here. Then, starting at the top of the puff pastry, and leaving about a ½-inch edge, arrange the slices, nicely overlapping, in whatever attractive pattern you feel like. Brush the fruit with the melted butter, and sprinkle with the sugar.
5. Put the tart in the oven and immediately turn the oven heat down to 375°F. Bake for 20 to 25 minutes, checking occasionally to poke down any renegade bubbles of pastry that might be forming at the center. Bake until the crust is quite golden brown and the peaches have caramelized a little. Be brave—you don't want carbon, but the flavor and texture are best when it's thoroughly cooked.

SPECIAL EQUIPMENT: *Parchment paper comes in handy here. You can find it in the supermarket aisle, with the tinfoil and the trash bags.*
TIME: *About 45 minutes total, but only about 15 minutes active time*
FEEDS: *10, easily. This is also great for breakfast the next day.*

Other fruits that work on this tart:

NOT ON LOVE ALONE

THREE BASIL PASTAS

Here's your revenge on those who would sell you too much basil—any one of these pastas uses up basil by the handful.

To store basil, I suggest treating it like lettuce: wash it, spin it dry in a salad spinner, then wrap it in a layer of paper towel and stow it in the crisper compartment of your refrigerator. Not as picturesque as it would be in a glass pitcher on your windowsill—but it will last a lot longer.

⤙ A NOTE ON PASTA ⤚

I AM A full supporter of dried pasta, particularly when you can get your hands on some of the more artisanal brands out there. They're more expensive than that 99-cent box of Ronzoni, but not by much, and they're much more flavorful. I like Latini, which comes in a chic brick-red box.

What I am not a fan of is that weirdly chemical, soft "fresh" pasta in the refrigerator case. It's sticky and unpleasantly thick. If you want fresh pasta, you might have to make it yourself. But that's a lesson for another day. In the meantime, stick with the high-quality dried kind.

Fusilli with Zucchini, Garlic, and Basil

This is the ultimate weekday pasta, as it has barely any components and it's very quickly done in the time the pasta takes to cook.

3 medium zucchini, washed and sliced into ¼-inch-square matchsticks, about 2½ inches long

Kosher salt

1-lb. box fusilli, or other twisted pasta

⅓ cup olive oil

3 cloves garlic, finely minced

1 handful fresh basil leaves, washed and dried

Sea salt and pepper

1 squeeze of fresh lemon juice, to taste

A generous amount of freshly grated Parmesan cheese, for the top

1. Fill the pasta pot and put it on to boil. While it's coming up to temperature, prepare the zucchini. Place the zucchini in a sieve or colander and salt it generously with kosher salt—a tablespoon should do—giving it a good toss. Set the sieve over a bowl and let the squash sit there for 15 minutes, to let it sweat.
2. When the water is boiling, add a palmful of kosher salt and then the pasta.
3. Place the oil and the chopped garlic in a cold, large frying pan, then cook it over medium heat until the little specks of garlic are dancing and perfuming your whole kitchen. Add the salted zucchini, turn up the heat to medium-high, and sauté, taking extra care to scrape up any garlic that otherwise might get stuck to the bottom and burn. You want the zucchini cooked through and relaxed, and this will take the entire rest of the pasta cooking time, about 7 minutes.
4. When the pasta is done, drain it and add it to the pan with the zucchini. Toss to combine (it might be easier to use two wooden spoons here, like salad tongs), then turn out onto a serving dish. Tear up the basil with your hands and add the leaves to the bowl. Give the hot pasta a bit more seasoning with sea salt and pepper and a squeeze of lemon. Toss once more, then add a heap of Parmesan cheese.

SPECIAL EQUIPMENT: *A pasta pot with a removable colander to drain it is a very easy way to handle hot pasta; it drains the water back into the pot rather than you having to struggle with pouring boiling pasta water down the sink.*
TIME: *10 minutes*
FEEDS: *4, generously (this is easily halved)*

NOT ON LOVE ALONE

Farfalle with Ricotta, Lemon, Basil, and Peas

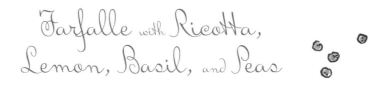

This pasta, a bit more complicated than the previous, gets its creaminess from ricotta cheese. Of course you can use the sort of ricotta that comes in the plastic bin, but if you're of a mind, try the fresh ricotta at the cheese counter. It has a smokier flavor and a firmer texture, a real counterpoint to the sweetness of the peas.

Though I haven't here, you might consider frying up a strip or two of bacon and adding it to the pasta at the end for a bit of salty punch.

Kosher salt

1 lb. dried farfalle (bowties) or other pasta with nooks and crannies

4 tablespoons unsalted butter

Finely grated zest of 1 lemon, plus the juice of half

1 cup frozen sweet peas

Sea salt and freshly ground black pepper

½ cup basil, rinsed and dried, finely chopped

1 cup ricotta, preferably whole-milk

A heap of freshly grated Parmesan cheese

1. Bring a pot of water to a boil. Add a palmful of kosher salt and the pasta to the water.
2. In the meantime, in a large skillet, melt the butter over a low flame. Add the lemon zest.
3. When the pasta has about 1 minute left to go, add the peas, lemon juice, and a good pinch of sea salt to the skillet, turning up the heat to medium-high. You just want to warm the peas through. Drain the pasta and add it to the skillet, and toss to combine. Slide everything into a serving bowl; then add the basil. Add the ricotta, dotting it about rather than adding it in one huge blob, which doesn't facilitate even distribution. Toss again, taste for salt, add some freshly ground pepper, then top with Parmesan cheese and serve.

TIME: *Just the time for the farfalle to cook, about 12 minutes*
FEEDS: *4 generously, but this can easily be halved.*

Spaghetti Pesto with Croutons

This is my favorite basil pasta recipe, and no wonder—it's the classic. For a while, I got very tired of pesto. It seemed as if it was smeared all over every sandwich, pizza, and piece of chicken I saw. But it's really very good, and best if made at home.

The croutons are a replacement for a very traditional pasta pesto accompaniment, potatoes. These croutons act as wicks for all the strong flavors, so when you get one, it's a burst of garlicky crunch in your mouth.

This recipe feeds four, but even when it's just the two of us I make the whole thing. It's surprising how much goes down the hatch in one sitting, and then I have leftovers to make a pasta pesto fritatta, which I serve the next night for dinner alongside a large green salad.

Kosher salt

1-lb. spaghetti

FOR THE PESTO:

Heaping 2 cups of fresh basil leaves, no stems, rinsed and dried

½ cup fresh flat-leaf parsley leaves, rinsed and dried

¼ cup pine nuts, toasted (see note)

2 large cloves garlic, sliced

½ cup olive oil

Heaping ½ cup freshly grated Parmesan cheese

FOR THE CROUTONS:

2 tablespoons olive oil

1½ cups of 1-inch cubes cut from a loaf of country bread, preferably a day old

1. Bring a pot of water to a boil. Add a palmful of kosher salt. While it's coming up to the boil, prep your ingredients. When it's there, add the spaghetti.
2. In the meantime, toss the following ingredients into the bowl of your food processor or blender: the basil, parsley, pine nuts, and garlic. Whiz about for a few moments to break down the bulk. (In a blender, you might add a tablespoon or two of water to facilitate this.) Then, through the pour spout on the top of either machine, add the olive oil in a thin stream until the mixture is bright green and emulsified. Pour it out into a serving bowl that's large enough to hold all the pasta. Mix in the Parmesan cheese with a spoon.
3. Heat the 2 tablespoons of olive oil in a frying pan over medium-high heat, and when it's shimmering, add the bread cubes, stirring them with a spatula or flipping them over in the pan with a flick of your wrist (someone should probably

show you how to do this before you attempt it on your own, but it's fun). When they're nicely toasted on one or two sides, slide them out onto some waiting paper towels, which will absorb the excess oil.

4. By this point, your spaghetti will be perfectly cooked. Drain it and add it to the pesto in the serving bowl, tossing it like a salad to evenly distribute. Add the croutons and toss again. Serve piping hot with more Parmesan cheese on the side. After you're done eating, try not to breathe on your neighbor.

NOTE: *To toast the pine nuts, place them in a dry pan over medium-low heat, stirring occasionally, until they are fragrant and golden brown.*

SPECIAL EQUIPMENT: *A blender or food processor is de rigueur.*
TIME: *Almost none at all for the pesto; altogether, as long as it takes the pasta to cook, about 8 minutes, plus a few minutes for prep and boiling water*
FEEDS: *4*

Fromage!
a Cheese Play in Five Acts

ACT FOUR: *The Hard Italians*

SCENE: *Again, the holy temple of Bleecker Street cheese, Murray's Cheese Shop. J stands before a large bin of cheese wedges, propped on top of a large wheel of Parmesan. JS stands by patiently.*

J, *confused.* Maybe I should get this one? (*She holds up a hefty wedge of Parmigiano Reggiano.*) Is this too much cheese?

JS, *looking at J as if she's crazy.* How's it different from this one here? (*He squints to read the label.*) It's organic Parmigiano Reggiano. It's rarer.

J. And more expensive. (*She sighs.*) Maybe I'll just get some Pecorino Romano for the tang. And some regular Parmesan.

JS. Is that enough? (*He starts to peer into the refrigerated case.*) I think we should get some other cheeses, as long as we're here . . .

(*black out*)

OCTOBER

Rabbit Stew vs. Rabbit Food

Rabbit Stew vs. Rabbit Food

JS WAS A little apprehensive the first time he ate rabbit, but after one bite the Easter bunny was forgotten forever. Rabbit is flavorful, leaner than chicken, and creates a spot of interest in an otherwise dreary sea of chicken cutlets and turkey burgers. It does well with bold accompaniments, as in the recipe I've included here, which is a tribute to a dish we had at our friend Ronny's house.

And while some people, like Ronny, feed us rabbit, we feed others vegetarian feasts. Our friend Kristin is a vegan with a capital V. Actually, you can just capitalize all those letters with Kristin. So JS dared me to make a vegan meal, and while I didn't delve into the mysterious world of tempeh and protein powders, I did a credible (if not totally nutritionally balanced) job. The second menu is merely vegetarian, not vegan, but I suggest some radical alterations if you, too, want to go all the way.

Ronny's Rabbit Tribute

RABBIT AND TOMATO STEW (PAGE 172)

&

LES CRÊPES CÉLÈBRE DE MÈRE BLANC (PAGE 176)

&

BAKED PEARS WITH BROWN SUGAR (PAGE 178)

~

Rabbit Food

FALL VEGETABLES WITH HOLLANDAISE SAUCE (PAGE 180)

&

ORECCHIETTE WITH LENTILS, BUTTERNUT SQUASH,
AND CREAM (PAGE 182)

&

SAUTÉED APPLES WITH VANILLA (PAGE 185)

RONNY'S RABBIT TRIBUTE

Rabbit and Tomato Stew

Our friends Ronny and Isabelle are avid and excellent home cooks. While they can both whip up a mean meal, they don't play well together in the kitchen. I guess I should say that Ronny doesn't play well with Isabelle in the kitchen. When he's cooking, he's a rock, an island, a gladiator locked in a one-on-one battle with his stove. Meanwhile, Isabelle rolls her eyes.

One time, Ronny came up with a terrific braised-rabbit recipe, and had us guess the ingredients. I picked up the cinnamon, and Ronny helpfully pointed out the brightness of the orange. When I begged him for the recipe, he shrugged his shoulders and said he had made it up. So this is my made-up version of Ronny's made-up recipe, a tribute to the original lost to history.

1 rabbit, cut up into serving pieces (ask your butcher—he might need to order this for you, or already have it frozen on hand; just ask him to cut it up for you)

3 tablespoons all-purpose flour

Kosher salt and pepper

2 tablespoons olive oil

2 cloves garlic

1 large yellow onion, chopped

1 stalk celery, minced

1 medium carrot, peeled and cut into thin rounds

1 sprig of fresh thyme

1 cinnamon stick, broken in half

2 cups canned whole plum tomatoes, with their juice

Zest of ½ orange

4 tablespoons freshly squeezed orange juice—less than ½ orange

Handful of chopped fresh flat-leaf parsley

1. Rinse off the rabbit and pat it dry with paper towels.
2. Put the flour on a plate and season it with some salt and pepper. Heat the olive oil over a medium flame in the bottom of the cast-iron casserole. When the oil is hot, brown the rabbit: Roll it in the flour piece by piece, knocking off any

excess, and lay it gently in the pot. Don't crowd the pan—plan on doing at least two batches. Sear the rabbit on both sides, about 4 minutes a side. Regulate the heat to keep the flour from burning. Reserve the browned rabbit on a platter.

3. When the rabbit's browned, add the garlic and onion to the pot. Stir until you can smell the garlic, then add a good pinch of salt. Sauté, stirring for a few minutes, until the onion has gone translucent. Add the celery and the carrot. Stir around, cooking until there's good color on the vegetables, about 10 minutes.

4. At this point, add the thyme and the cinnamon stick. Let them swirl in the fat, then add the rabbit back into the pot and top with the 2 cups of plum tomatoes. (I always cut up the tomatoes on their way into the pot by using my kitchen scissors.) Give the contents of the pot a stir, look for a few heat bubbles, then cover the casserole tightly and turn down the heat to a minimum. Go do something else for a while.

5. Occasionally, you can stir things in the pot, just to make sure it's not cooking too fast, and to make sure nothing is sticking. But it should braise, almost undisturbed, for 2½ hours. At that point, take off the lid and inspect your stew. Beautiful, no? The cinnamon makes it smell terrific. Now, add the orange zest and the bit of orange juice that you reserved. Stir it around, then cover again and continue cooking for 30 minutes.

6. The rabbit should be done then, so tender that it's almost falling off the bones. Taste for salt and pepper. You can serve it right away with a sprinkling of parsley, or you can let it stand and gently reheat it before serving.

SPECIAL EQUIPMENT: *Just a large casserole, such as a Le Creuset*
TIME: *More than 3 hours, mostly unattended*
FEEDS: *4 to 6*

Rabbit and Game

M<small>Y</small> BUTCHER SHOP, Ottomanelli's, specializes in game, so no matter what fancy strikes me, they probably have it in the back, just waiting for me. A rabbit is child's play. Pheasant? Not a problem. Quail? Of course. For a while, they would tease me by asking if I needed any squab today, as I was deep into a Moroccan pigeon pie phase and seemed to be buying some every week. They even have some elk jerky on their stainless-steel counter, waiting for the day when somebody wants to eat elk jerky.

If you don't live down the block from Ottomanelli's, your game whims might have to wait for delivery from specialized butchers elsewhere. But don't you want to try cooking venison, at least once? Of course, I recommend buying any mail-order game from Ottomanelli's, at www.ottomanellimeats.com.

Sometimes game comes from actual game hunters. A friend of ours named CD, a sensitive, quiet soul and doctoral candidate in art history (perhaps we should call him Dr. CD), is also from Texas, wears cowboy boots, and goes pheasant hunting. One time he sent over a brace of pheasants for me to cook for a dinner party. The preparation involved a pair of needle-nosed pliers and a small knife to remove the shot. I had a great time.

QUAIL

SQUAB

VENISON LOIN

What Is Mirepoix?

$\mathcal{B}$EFORE SITTING DOWN to write this book, I knew what mirepoix was, but I had no idea what its origin was. It's French, and for some reason I thought the name had something to do with peas (because *pois* is the French word for peas). It made a sort of convoluted sense because you dice the components of mirepoix, perhaps into pea-size pieces. Voilà!

However, I was tragically wrong. Mirepoix, according to the *Larousse Gastronomique*, is named after Monsieur Mirepoix, who was the first one to come up with the standard proportions of 2 parts onion to 1 part carrot and 1 part celery. Thousands of dishes start off this way, so Monsieur Mirepoix was on to something.

ONION

CELERY

CARROT

Les Crêpes Célèbre de Mère Blanc

his is a venerable French recipe, a potato cake from the wise and all-knowing Mother White.
Who was Mother White, you ask? Beats me. But try these crepes, and I think you'll agree that
Mother White, whoever she was, knew what she was doing.

These can also be served for dessert, if you want to dust them with sugar and put them under
a fruit compote, or serve them with some other sweet thing.

1 lb. starchy potatoes, such as russets

4 egg whites

4 tablespoons all-purpose flour

3 whole eggs

1½ teaspoons kosher salt

3 tablespoons heavy cream or crème fraîche

Clarified butter, for cooking (see note)

1. Peel the potatoes, cut them into large, uniform chunks, and put them in a pot with cold water. Bring the water to a boil and cook the spuds until they're tender, about 15 minutes. Drain, then immediately puree the potatoes into a large mixing bowl, using either a potato ricer (to work out your forearms) or a food mill (for your biceps). Let the potatoes cool for a minute or two.
2. In the meantime, in a smaller bowl, whisk the egg whites just until the albumen is broken up a little bit.
3. Back to the potatoes: Mix in the flour with a wooden spoon, then the whole eggs, one at a time. This will be looking decidedly gloopy. Then, add the egg whites in dribs and drabs, until all the eggs are finally incorporated. Throw in the salt and the bit of cream. The mixture should have the consistency of vanilla pudding.
4. Heat a large skillet or griddle over lively heat, and pour on a few teaspoons of clarified butter (watch out, it might spatter). Drop the potato mixture by soup-spoonfuls into the hot pan. The little crepes will spread and form all by themselves. Give them a minute or two to brown on one side, then flip them and brown on the other. They'll be the shape and color of silver-dollar pancakes. You can drain them on paper towels while you continue cooking, adding more clarified butter as necessary. I always like to make some deliberate "mistakes" so I, as the chef, will be forced to eat one. Or two. Try not to eat all the crepes before your guests arrive!

NOT ON LOVE ALONE

NOTE: *These crepes need to be cooked in clarified butter, which is easy to make. Simply melt a stick of butter in the top of a double boiler, then spoon off the milk solids that float to the top, pour off the clear, yellow butter, and discard the impurities that have sunk to the bottom. Unused clarified butter will keep in the fridge for a couple of weeks.*

SPECIAL EQUIPMENT: *A potato ricer or a food mill, to puree the potatoes and remove any lumps. (A food processor is vehemently not recommended—it makes potatoes gummy.) A roomy frying pan, or even a griddle, for ease of flipping, would also be nice.*

TIME: *About 1 hour, but you can make them ahead and reheat them in a low oven at serving time.*

FEEDS: *If you estimate 5 pancakes per person, about 6.*

⚝ A MAN'S UTENSIL ⚝

The Potato Ricer

ONCE, FOR CHRISTMAS, my cousin Patty gave JS an unusual gift. It was a potato ricer. Understandably confused, JS held it in the air for a moment, blinking, and said a perplexed thank-you. But Patty clarified. She told him that all good Irish households had a potato ricer, for making smooth mashed potatoes, and that it was the man's job to deal with the grunt work of squeezing the boiled potatoes through the ricer's tiny holes. JS is not one to shirk his responsibility. I should note that this remains JS's only active cooking duty to date.

POTATOES IN HERE

CLOSE TO
PUSH THROUGH

Baked Pears with Brown Sugar

This is a perfect fall dessert—and you can feel virtuous for eating fruit.

4 Bosc pears, peeled

2 tablespoons unsalted butter

4 tablespoons brown sugar

A drizzle of maple syrup
(the real sort, please)

1. Preheat the oven to 350°F.
2. Core the pears: attacking them from the bottom with a teaspoon, scoop out all the seeds and the fibrous heart of the pears, trying not to pierce the pear anywhere but the bottom as you do so. This takes a few minutes.
3. Have a rimmed baking sheet or little roasting pan ready. Take a pear, put ½ tablespoon of butter and 1 full tablespoon of brown sugar in the cavity, and stand it up on its end on the baking sheet. Do this with its friends. Once the pears are ready to go, drizzle the tops with some maple syrup and add a few drops of water to the bottom of the pan to keep the sugar from burning.
4. Bake for 25 to 30 minutes, depending on the ripeness of the pears (less time for riper pears), until the pears are soft, and the sugar is nice and runny. You can serve these right out of the oven, or just warm, and you can add some whipped cream if you're feeling decadent.

TIME: *30 minutes*
FEEDS: *4, but this is easily halved (or multiplied)*

❧ TARTING UP BAKED FRUIT ❧

*N*O BAKED FRUIT need remain unstuffed! Anything you want can go in the cavity for a bit of a dessert surprise. Chopped toasted pecans, golden raisins, a bit of chopped, candied ginger, or semisweet chocolate chips all add a bit of fun to the brown sugar and butter filling.

RABBIT FOOD

OF COURSE, THERE are those who won't eat rabbit stew, or any-thing else containing something that once walked on the earth. Some of these people are dear friends, and we call them vegetarians.

I embrace a good vegetarian meal, though I'm less happy with a vegan one, so the menu below is really vegetarian—for those who will eat cheese and eggs. But the hollandaise could easily be replaced by a robust vinaigrette, and you can serve the pasta without any cheese, or with cheese on the side for those who want it. I wouldn't tweak the sautéed apples, because the butter is irreplaceable, but you can ask the vegan guest of honor to bring along some sorbet for everyone.

Fall Vegetables with Hollandaise Sauce

The idea here is to gather as many colors, textures, and flavors you can get on one platter, then arrange them like a Dutch still life, with the sauce on the side.

FOR THE VEGETABLES:

3 red beets, trimmed

5 small golden beets, trimmed

1 pint Brussels sprouts

1 bulb fennel

1 bunch broccoli rabe

½ head cauliflower

1 bunch scallions

¼ lb. purple Peruvian potatoes

1 half-pint red pearl onions

2 tender hearts of celery, with leaves

½ cup vegetable stock, more as needed

2 stemmed portobello mushrooms

Olive oil as needed

Sea salt

FOR THE HOLLANDAISE:

3 egg yolks

1 teaspoon fresh lemon juice, or to taste

Sea salt and black pepper

1 stick unsalted butter, melted and kept hot

1. The beets, Brussels sprouts, and fennel should be steamed. (You should probably steam the beets in a large pot and do the Brussels sprouts and fennel in batches in a separate pot.) Prepare the vegetables as follows:

Beets: Steam large beets for up to 40 minutes; smaller beets from 20 to 30 minutes. They're done when a knife tip slides in easily, as into a potato. Peel the cooked beets with a vegetable peeler or paring knife and cut them into thick wedges for serving.

Brussels Sprouts: Keep the sprouts whole and cut an X into the bottom of each one with a paring knife. Steam them for about 10 minutes, so they're a bit tender but still retain their bright color. Run them under cold water to stop the cooking.

Fennel: Trim off most of the fronds and tops of the bulb, cut the bulb into sixths, and trim the core. Drizzle with a tiny bit of olive oil, then steam for 10 to 12 minutes, until the outer layers become tender and a bit translucent.

NOT ON LOVE ALONE

2. The broccoli rabe, cauliflower, scallions, onions, and purple potatoes can be boiled, in batches, in the same pot. Place a large pot of salted water to boil over high heat, and prepare the vegetables as follows:

   Broccoli Rabe: Drop the broccoli rabe, bottom stems trimmed, into the rapidly boiling salted water for 2 to 4 minutes, then run it under cold water to stop the cooking.

   Cauliflower: Trim the cauliflower into medium-large dramatic florets. Cook the florets in the boiling water for 5 to 7 minutes, then run them under cold water to stop the cooking. You want them to be tender, with a bit of resistance.

   Scallions: Trim the ends, then blanch the scallions for two minutes in the boiling water. Drain, and rinse under cold water.

   Purple Potatoes: Boil them whole in their skins, in salted water, about 10 minutes (or longer for larger ones). Let cool, then peel and slice into wedges.

   Pearl Onions: While the potatoes are cooling, drop unpeeled pearl onions into the boiling water for 8 to 10 minutes. Cool them with cold water, slice off the root end, and squeeze to peel.

3. Cut the hearts of celery in half lengthwise down the middle, and lay them flat in a skillet. Add ½ cup vegetable stock, bring to a simmer, put the lid on slightly ajar, and cook for 10 minutes, or until the bottom of the celery is easily pierced with a knife.

4. Brush the mushrooms lightly with olive oil and lightly sauté them in a nonstick pan, about 3 minutes a side.

5. Arrange the vegetables on a platter and, right before serving, make the hollandaise: Blend together the egg yolks, lemon juice, and good pinches of salt and pepper. Then, keeping the machine running, pour the hot butter through the pour spout on the top in a very thin stream, stretching it out for about a minute. The hollandaise should be thickened at the end of a minute. Taste for seasoning and lemon, then pour into a serving bowl.

SPECIAL EQUIPMENT: *A food processor or hand blender*
TIME: *About 2 hours*
FEEDS: *This feast serves 6 to 8 as a hearty first course or main course.*

Orecchiette with Lentils, Butternut Squash, and Cream

This is a slightly unusual dish, but the earthiness of the lentils and the freshness of the squash really play well off one another. The bread crumbs add another textural element without much effort.

2 tablespoons unsalted butter

½ cup dried plain bread crumbs

Kosher salt

2 tablespoons olive oil

⅓ cup red onion or shallot, diced fine

2 cloves garlic, minced

¼ cup finely diced carrot

¼ cup finely diced celery

pinch of ground cumin

1 sprig of fresh thyme

⅓ cup dried Le Puy lentils (you can substitute brown lentils in a pinch)

1½ cup vegetable stock (or chicken stock)

1 lb. dried orecchiette pasta

1 cup peeled and diced butternut squash (pieces should be ¼ inch)

Black pepper, to taste

Pinch of hot pepper flakes (optional)

5 tablespoons heavy cream

Parmesan cheese for grating over the top

1. In a small frying pan, melt 1 tablespoon of the butter and, when the foam has subsided, add the bread crumbs. Toast over medium heat for a minute or two; set aside.

2. Put a pot of water on to boil for the pasta. Add a palmful of kosher salt. While the water is coming up to temperature, prepare the vegetables and heat a large frying pan on the stove. Add the olive oil, heat for a moment, then add the red onion and garlic. Add a pinch of kosher salt. Sauté until the red onion relaxes and starts to become translucent, about 3 minutes. Then, add the carrot and celery, sautéing well for at least 5 minutes more.

3. At this point, add the cumin and thyme to the pan and stir to combine. Then add the lentils, swirling them around so they're covered in the oil. Add the 1½ cups of stock (you could also substitute 1½ cups of water), bring to the boil, and then lower the heat to a minimum. The lentils will take about 12 minutes to cook.

4. After the lentils have been cooking for 3 minutes, pop the orecchiette into the water. Check the package, but they'll probably take about 10 minutes to cook. Check your lentils—they should be soupy until the end of the cooking time. If they're looking dry, add a few tablespoons of water and turn down the heat.

5. When the lentils have been cooking for 10 minutes total, add the diced butternut squash. The squash cooks very quickly and you want it to retain its color, so don't add it too early. Add salt and pepper to taste, and the pinch of hot pepper, if you like it. Test the lentils to check their doneness. They should be tender but still have some character to them.

6. As the pasta is nearing the perfect al dente stage, the lentils should have absorbed all their liquid and be cooked through. Add the cream and stir, then turn off the heat and swirl in the remaining tablespoon of butter. Drain the pasta and add it to the skillet, stirring to combine. Transfer the lot to a serving bowl, sprinkle with the buttered bread crumbs, and grate a generous amount of Parmesan cheese over the top.

TIME: *20 minutes*
FEEDS: *6*

Dinner-Party Food on the Fly

I REMEMBER COOKING a five-course meal for my parents' thirtieth wedding anniversary a few years ago. When the guests were about five minutes from sitting down, an old friend of my parents' came in and whispered to me that her husband was lactose-intolerant, so could I remove any dairy from his portions please? Eeek!

As a cook who likes to entertain, the most important thing to be is flexible. Most people will eat what's put down in front of them, even if it's something they might not make themselves. Sometimes, you might broaden their palates an inch or two. But sometimes it's only gracious to try and accommodate someone who can't eat what you've made, particularly if it's because of a health or religious issue.

So what did I do for my father's guest, his dearest friend from college? I gave him caviar on toast points, when everyone else was having a lemon pot de crème with caviar; I tossed his homemade pasta with herbs and olive oil when everyone else got a bit of cream sauce before the white truffles went on top; I skated through the main course, blessedly dairy-free; and then I let him decide if he wanted to risk the buttercream icing on the celebration cake. All in all, about five minutes of extra work ensured a successful lactose-free meal.

Sautéed Apples with Vanilla

This is lovely on its own—it's basically tarte tatin without the tarte part—but it really shines as a topping. I particularly recommend serving these apples with two recipes featured elsewhere in the book—the Lace Cookies on page 21, and the Pastry Cream filling for the éclairs on page 220. If you serve them with cookies, all the apples need in addition is some lightly sweetened whipped cream. The pastry cream is perfect on its own, but with one crucial alteration to the recipe— reduce the cornstarch from one-quarter cup to two tablespoons. You want a silkier, more relaxed pudding than you would need as a filling for pastry.

4 tablespoons unsalted butter

4 Gala apples, peeled, cored, and each cut into 12 wedges

4 tablespoons sugar

½ vanilla bean, split

2 tablespoons fresh lemon juice

1. Melt the butter in a roomy skillet over medium-high heat. When the foam has subsided, add the apples, the sugar, the split vanilla pod, and 1 tablespoon of the lemon juice. Shake the pan to combine.
2. Continue to cook over lively heat, keeping an eye on the pan and shaking it vigorously from time to time, for about 20 minutes, or until the sugar has caramelized and turned the apples a lovely clear amber-brown. Turn the apples out into a serving bowl, remove the vanilla pods, and add the rest of the lemon juice, to taste.

TIME: *30 minutes*
FEEDS: *4 to 6, depending on how you use it*

NOVEMBER

Home for the Holidays

Home for the Holidays

AIRPLANE FOOD IS typically some of the most repulsive in the world. The haute cuisine of the friendly skies is only the worst offender; the microwaved "sandwiches" in the Amtrak Northeast Corridor bar cars manage to be both slimy and dry at the same time; and the anemic burgers at the Arby's in rest stops along the New Jersey Turnpike are only good for a bad case of heartburn around about Baltimore. I know this, for I have eaten them all.

But, a few years ago, I was introduced to travel food done right. JS and I went to Japan for three weeks so he could watch the World Cup and I could eat all the Japanese food I could, all day long. One of the most amusing foodie delights was the cornucopia of bento boxes to be purchased at train stations (or from a food cart on the train itself). Ranging in price and variety, filled with sushi, seaweed salads, or noodles, these clever lunch boxes were chicer and better tasting than anything on this side of the Pacific. I had to have one on every train ride, hungry or not.

So, I've faked up a bento box in time for the Thanksgiving holidays, for when every newly married couple is making its way to his parents or hers. Believe me when I tell you you'll feel much better after eating this than you would that tragic hot dog that's been rotating under the heat lamp for two hours.

On the other end, I've included some light, quick soups to make—nary a turkey scrap in sight—when you're back home repenting your gluttonous ways. They're soothing and delicious, perfect for lifting your turkey stupor.

For the Plane, Train, or Automobile

FRITTATA WRAP (PAGE 190)

&

EDAMAME (PAGE 192)

&

FENNEL AND RADISH SALAD (PAGE 193)

&

SOMETHING EXTRA: CARROT SOUFFLÉ (PAGE 195)

Thanksgiving Detox

EGG DROP SOUP WITH MINT (PAGE 197)

&

CAULIFLOWER SOUP WITH CUMIN SEEDS AND PARSLEY (PAGE 198)

&

CHICKEN SOUP WITH GINGER, BARLEY, AND CHESTNUTS (PAGE 199)

⌒

Frittata Wrap

This is a take on a sushi roll, using tortilla wraps (or lavash, as you prefer), but you could always be more conventional and sandwich the frittata between layers of ciabatta or even a crusty baguette.

1 cup cooked sushi rice (prepared according to package directions and cooled)

2 teaspoons rice wine or white wine vinegar

1 scallion, sliced thinly on the bias, white and light green parts only

2 teaspoons sesame seeds

4 eggs, lightly beaten

½ teaspoon kosher salt

1½ teaspoons sugar

2 teaspoons unsalted butter

2 whole-wheat or spinach sandwich wraps

4 tablespoons softened cream cheese

4 ounces smoked salmon, thinly sliced

1. In a medium-size mixing bowl, combine the rice with the rice wine vinegar, then mix in the scallion and sesame seeds. You can do this with your hands, but that rice is awfully sticky.
2. Add the eggs, salt, and sugar, and mix to combine.
3. Heat a nonstick pan over medium heat, melt the butter, and swirl it about to cover the whole bottom. Pour in the egg mixture, making sure it's distributed evenly, then cover the pan and turn the heat down to medium low. Let the frittata cook, undisturbed, for 10 minutes.
4. After 10 minutes, check the eggs. The omelet should be completely firm on top and golden along the edges. Turn off the heat, and then upend the frittata onto a cutting board and let cool.
5. When the frittata is cool, cut it into inch-wide long strips. Take a sandwich wrap and spread it with a thin layer of cream cheese. (Scallion cream cheese would also

be good here, or, if you don't want to use the smoked salmon, a cream cheese with olives. Or you could nix the cream cheese altogether and use a smooth hummus. That could have olives, too. You get the picture.) Top with a few thin slices of salmon in a single layer.

6. Finish assembling the sandwich: Layer some strips of the frittata in a square in the center of the sandwich wrap, making sure to leave enough wrap free to fold up and roll the sandwich. Then, with the strips facing you horizontally, fold up the near edge of the bread over the frittata, fold the sides in, and roll up. The goal here is to wrap it like a burrito—a simple process, only somewhat convoluted when put into words.

7. Cut the sandwich in half, line the halves up next to each other, and wrap tightly in plastic wrap. Repeat steps 5 through 7 for the second sandwich. Keep in the fridge until you're ready to go.

SPECIAL EQUIPMENT: *A nonstick omelet pan is essential here.*
TIME: *About 20 minutes, not including time to cook the rice*
FEEDS: *2 hungry travelers*

⌁ SHOPPING FROM THE NEWSSTAND ∾

*T*HIS IS WHAT you should buy instead of that cylinder of Sour Cream & Onion Pringles:

Cashew nuts
Pistachios
Dried apricots
Trail mix
Peanut M&M's

Edamame

These fresh soybeans, aka Japanese beer nuts, are widely available in the freezer section now, and they're ridiculously easy to make. Just bring some salted water to a boil and add the frozen edamame. After the water has come back to the boil, cook the edamame for three minutes, drain them, run them under cool water, and then shell them. Sprinkle them generously with salt, and keep in the refrigerator until you're ready to head out.

⌒ OTHER BENTO BOXERS ⌒

Roasted, salted pumpkin seeds
Home-popped popcorn
Cherry tomatoes
Wasabi peas
Smoked almonds
Japanese rice crackers

EDAMAME

SANDWICH

RADISH
-and-
FENNEL

PURLOINED
FORK

Fennel and Radish Salad

This is refreshing and very easy to make. Just store the salad in a disposable plastic container and bring along a plastic fork (or procure one from the Amtrak bar car).

1 small bulb fennel

5 or 6 radishes

A squeeze of fresh lemon juice, to taste
(about ½ lemon)

A drizzle of good olive oil

Sea salt and pepper

Trim, wash, and dry the fennel, and trim and wash the radishes. Cut the fennel in half and run each half through the mandoline. Do the same with the radishes. Put both into a plastic container with a lid, add the lemon juice and olive oil, and salt and pepper to taste. Mix, and stick in the fridge until it's time to leave.

SPECIAL EQUIPMENT: *This salad is this salad because of a mandoline. The plastic varieties are cheap and endlessly useful.*
TIME: *2 minutes, if you're slow*
FEEDS: *2*

Something Extra

$\mathscr{A}$ WORD TO the wise. It pays to arrive for any holiday at your in-laws' house well-armed with a recipe you can prepare for the assembled masses. This carrot soufflé is particularly good because it requires so little time in the kitchen, and yet you can do so much with it. That way, you're helpful and thoughtful, but you don't get in the way while your mother-in-law roasts the turkey or worries about the stuffing.

The best part is that the soufflé looks sophisticated and impressive, but is a snap to make. Plus, if you anticipate that the kitchen on Turkey Day afternoon will closely resemble O'Hare International Airport, you can make the soufflé in the morning and reheat it in the already hot oven for about ten minutes just before serving.

Carrot Soufflé

his is a Carry family tradition that originally came from our erstwhile upstairs neighbor, Betsy Newell.

3 slices white bread	3 eggs, beaten
1 cup milk	4 tablespoons grated Swiss cheese
7 carrots, boiled until tender	1 teaspoon kosher salt
2 tablespoons unsalted butter, melted	5 teaspoons sugar

1. Preheat the oven to 350°F.
2. Put the bread in a small bowl and cover with the milk. Let it soak for 5 minutes, until the bread has wicked up all the liquid.
3. Place the bread and the remaining ingredients in the bowl of a food processor. Blend them until you have a bright orange, uniform batter. An easy way to impress the in-laws, no?
4. Put the mixture into a greased soufflé dish. Prepare a bain-marie (see note), which will keep the bottom of your soufflé from scorching.
5. Bake the soufflé for 1 hour 10 minutes to 1 hour 15 minutes, or until the top is puffed and lightly golden. Serve piping hot.

NOTE: *To set up a bain-marie, boil some water in a kettle, put the soufflé dish (or other ceramic baking dish) in a roasting pan on the oven rack, and then pour the boiling water at least 1/2 inch up the sides of the soufflé dish. Then simply slide the rack back in the oven. (Trying to do this on the counter before transferring it to the oven is a great way to get scalded.)*

SPECIAL EQUIPMENT: *A blender or food processor*
TIME: *About 1 1/2 hours total, but much of that is unattended baking time.*
FEEDS: *Everyone at the Thanksgiving table*

THANKSGIVING DETOX

After the week o' turkey, it's time to turn over a new leaf, culinarily speaking. However, the turkey has made you so tired you can barely turn on the stove, never mind run out to the store and buy anything for dinner. Despite that, the mere idea of vats of grease delivered to your door courtesy of your local Chinese takeout makes you shudder.

My solution? Easy soups made from ingredients that are mostly on hand, or easily purchased before you leave for vacation.

Here is my own ersatz brand of Chinese-homeopathy-cum-old-wives'-tales of what makes you feel better when you eat it. Some of the ingredients—mint, cumin, ginger, star anise—clear your head and settle your stomach. So you're not only eating something yummy, you're eating something that's good for you. How great is that?

Egg Drop Soup with Mint

There's nothing simpler than this soup. With only four ingredients, it couldn't be faster or easier. My one whole-hearted recommendation is that you use real homemade chicken stock, which, I hope, is lurking in your freezer at this very moment. The taste of this soup is so pure that homemade stock really completes it. If homemade chicken stock is not in the cards, choose a low-sodium chicken stock, preferably one in a laminated box rather than a can—I think the canned variety develops a metallic tang as it sits on the shelf.

4 cups homemade chicken stock

2 eggs, lightly beaten

1½ teaspoons kosher salt (if using homemade stock, which is unsalted; if not, just add sea salt to taste at the end)

1 tablespoon chopped fresh mint

Sea salt

1. Bring the 4 cups of stock to a low boil in a medium-size saucepan. If using homemade stock, add the kosher salt. Turn down the heat to medium-low.
2. Pour the beaten eggs into the pot in a slow stream, whisking the entire time. The eggs will set up immediately, forming lacy webs in the soup. Turn off the heat.
3. Add the mint and the sea salt to taste. Pour into bowls and eat.

TIME: *5 minutes*

FEEDS: *2 people in need of revivification*

Cauliflower Soup
with Cumin Seeds and Parsley

Only slightly more complicated than the previous recipe, the trickiest part of this recipe is smashing the cooked cauliflower against the side of the pot with a wooden spoon.

1 teaspoon whole cumin seeds

2 teaspoons olive oil

1 shallot, minced

3 cups small cauliflower florets—less than a head of cauliflower

4 cups homemade chicken stock (boxed low-sodium stock can be substituted)

1½ teaspoons kosher salt (if using home-made stock, which is unsalted; if using boxed broth, taste for salt first)

1 tablespoon unsalted butter (optional)

2 tablespoons finely chopped flat-leaf parsley

Sea salt and pepper to taste

1. In a small frying pan, toast the cumin seeds over medium heat until they're fragrant. Spill them out onto the counter and bruise them slightly with the bottom of a glass or the side of a chef's knife.
2. Heat the oil over medium heat in a medium-size saucepan. Add the shallot and sauté until translucent, just 2 or 3 minutes. Add the cauliflower and chicken stock (and the kosher salt, if using premade broth) and bring to a boil. Cook the cauliflower for 10 minutes, until very soft. Turn the heat down to low and, using the back of a wooden spoon, break up some of the florets. You're certainly not trying to puree anything here, but just to make it feel more souplike.
3. Stir in the butter. When it's melted, add the cumin seeds and parsley, and taste for salt and pepper. Serve right away.

TIME: *15 minutes*
FEEDS: *2 tired travelers*

NOT ON LOVE ALONE

Chicken Soup
with Ginger, Barley, and Chestnuts

This is the most complicated of the soups, only because it has the most ingredients. But it's really quite easy to make, and the broth, perfumed with ginger and star anise, is addictive.

4 cups homemade chicken stock (boxed low-sodium stock can be substituted)

½ lb. skinned and boned chicken thighs (about 2 thighs)

2 tablespoons pearl barley

1½ teaspoons kosher salt (if using home-made stock, which is unsalted; if using premade broth, taste for salt first)

½ cup chestnuts, either canned or jarred (my preference)

1 teaspoon peeled, julienned fresh ginger

½ star anise

1 scallion, sliced thinly on the bias, white and light green parts only

Sea salt and pepper, to taste

A bit of Bartlett or Anjou pear, cut into matchsticks (optional, for garnish)

1. Place the stock, chicken, and barley in a medium saucepan over high heat. If using homemade stock, add the salt. As soon as it's at a gentle boil, cover the pot and reduce the heat to low. Let the chicken and barley cook, covered, for 30 minutes.
2. Uncover the pot and take a look inside. The barley should have blossomed and be almost tender. Fish the chicken thighs out and, using a fork or the tip of a paring knife, pull the thighs apart into medium-size chunks. The meat should come apart pretty easily. Return the meat to the soup pot.
3. Break the chestnuts into pieces with your fingers, and add them to the pot along with the ginger, star anise, and scallion. Cook, uncovered, at a simmer for another 10 minutes.
4. Test for salt and pepper, then ladle into bowls. Add a few matchsticks of pear, if you're using it (I highly recommend it—the sweetness and tenderness bring out the ginger in the soup). Eat up as fast as you can spoon it into your mouth.

TIME: *45 minutes*
FEEDS: *2*

Winter Pantry

THERE ARE QUITE a few more must-haves in my winter pantry than in my summer pantry. I think this is because (a) it's cold outside and I don't want to have to run out to the store all the time, and (b) we eat more in the winter. Seriously, I think it's because, considering the ripeness of vegetables in the height of summer, you don't need to fuss with them so much. A bit of herb, a squeeze of lemon, and you're good to go. In the winter, a greater depth of flavor is called for. Here is a list of both straight pantry items and some vegetables that are always in my fridge:

Lentils: Both regular brown lentils and the tiny, moss-green Le Puy lentils make the cut.

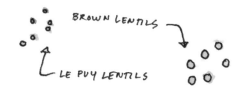

Dried Beans: Such as cannellini, kidney, garbanzo, and cranberry. For salads and hearty soups and stews.

Dried Mushrooms: Especially dried morels, which add such flavor to risotto and stews. Simply soak them in hot water and make sure they're free of sand.

Shredded Cabbage: I like red and Savoy cabbage, and it's easier to store shredded in resealable bags, ready to be sautéed or braised.

Brussels Sprouts: Maybe my favorite vegetable. Best way to prepare them? Sliced in half, sautéed with garlic and olive oil.

Hearty Greens: Such as kale or beet greens. I like to sauté them, much as I would Brussels sprouts, but you can also bake the stalks with Parmesan cheese.

Chestnuts: I prefer chestnuts that are vacuum-packed in jars, rather than the sort canned in water; they're firmer and more flavorful. You can use them in soups or roast them alongside pork spare ribs.

Interesting Root Vegetables: An occasional celery root, salsify, or parsnip will make its way home with me from the green market. They're great roasted next to meats.

DECEMBER

The Big Payback

The Big Payback

emember, once upon a time, you had friends. These were people you went to the movies with, ate at diners with, drank at dive bars with, and who, most recently, paid many bucks to schlep to your wedding, stay in the local Discomfort Inn, and complete your set of sterling-silver dinner forks.

Of course, you haven't seen them recently. You've been busy at home, buying a new hamper together, dealing with your new joint bank accounts, et cetera. But now, it's payback time. You have the new home. It's filled to choking with shiny new tchotchkes, and it's time to put them to good use. That's right. It's time to have a party.

The best sort of cocktail party to have at home is the party where your guests can graze, moving from cozy spot to cozy spot in your living room while sampling all the good eats. You can bring things out in waves: the nuts, chickpeas, and cheese puffs first, followed by the hot (or warm) hors d'oeuvres when the party gets rocking. Finally, when you want to signal that things should wind up soon, bring out dessert. Then bring out the wheelbarrow to cart your guests out the door.

Payback Party Eats

SPICED PECANS (PAGE 206)

SPICY CHICKPEAS (PAGE 207)

MINI MOROCCAN PASTILLAS (PAGE 208)

GOUGÈRES (CHEESE PUFFS) (PAGE 210)

FRIED VEGGIES (PAGE 214)

WATER CHESTNUTS WRAPPED IN BACON (PAGE 218)

CRÈME BRÛLÉE ECLAIRS (PAGE 220)

Winter Tipples

FORTIFIED PIMM'S (PAGE 224)

THE STINKING BISHOP (PAGE 225)

THE WEEKENDER (PAGE 227)

REAL TOM COLLINS (PAGE 227)

PAYBACK PARTY EATS

I like these with a little kick of heat—the half teaspoon of cayenne pepper is the high end of polite spiciness. If you want a tamer nut, use one-quarter teaspoon.

4 cups pecan halves

1 egg white

1 teaspoon kosher salt

1 tablespoon crushed, dried rosemary leaves

½ teaspoon cayenne pepper (or to taste)

½ teaspoon ground cumin

2 tablespoons light brown sugar

Nonstick cooking spray, to grease the sheet pan

1. Preheat the oven to 325°F.
2. Spread out the nuts in an even layer on a rimmed baking sheet, and pop them into the oven for 5 to 7 minutes, until lightly toasted.
3. Meanwhile, put the egg white in a medium-size mixing bowl and whisk lightly to break up the albumen. Add the salt, the spices and the sugar, and whisk to combine. When you remove the nuts from the oven, let them cool for a moment, then add them to the spice mixture and coat them evenly. Spray the cookie sheet with the nonstick cooking spray, put them back on the cookie sheet in an even layer and bake for another 20 to 22 minutes, until lacquered with the spices and a lovely mahogany brown. Let them cool before you serve them or transfer them to an airtight container.

TIME: *35 minutes*
FEEDS: *This recipe makes 4 cups of nuts, enough for 16 noshers.*

Not on Love Alone

Spicy Chickpeas

Here's another kick of heat: the more heat your snacks give off, the more people drink and the more festive your party becomes. Capisce? You can actually get a version of these at Indian grocery stores (that's how I first tried them), but making them at home is easy enough.

1 cup dried chickpeas	¼ teaspoon cayenne pepper
½ teaspoon curry powder	Pinch of kosher salt
¼ teaspoon paprika	Neutral vegetable oil (safflower or canola) for deep frying

1. Either soak the chickpeas in cold water overnight, or pour boiling water over them and soak for 1½ hours, depending on how much you've planned ahead. When they're softened, pat them dry thoroughly.
2. Fill a deep saucepan with vegetable oil about a third of the way up. Set up the frying thermometer so the probe is in the oil but not touching the sides or bottom of the pan. Heat the oil to 350°F. While it's heating, fill a rimmed baking sheet with a layer of crumpled paper towels.
3. Fry the chickpeas in batches, 3 minutes per batch. Scoop them out with a bamboo-handled strainer or a slotted spoon and let them drain on the paper towels. When you've done all the chickpeas, refry them in batches for another 3 minutes per batch, until slightly golden.
4. Drain the chickpeas again, then transfer them to a bowl. In another small bowl, combine the curry, paprika, cayenne pepper, and salt, then sprinkle this mixture over the chickpeas. Let cool, then serve.

SPECIAL EQUIPMENT: *A candy or frying thermometer, to monitor the hot oil*
TIME: *Some unattended time soaking the chickpeas, but only a few minutes of working time*
FEEDS: *Makes about 2 cups of chickpeas, enough for two dishes scattered about the party*

Mini Moroccan Pastillas

The most complicated recipe in this chapter, but it's stunning and easily made ahead. Everybody will think they're those tired old spinach-stuffed phyllo triangles and get a delicious surprise instead. JS has been known to eat half a batch in one sitting, before the guests arrive, pleasing himself if not his wife.

1 lb. skinless, boneless chicken thighs

1 clove garlic, minced

¼ cup finely chopped fresh flat-leaf parsley

1 shallot, minced

A pinch of saffron

¼ teaspoon ground ginger

½ teaspoon ground cinnamon

1 stick unsalted butter

½ cup water

Pinch of kosher salt and pepper

2 eggs, lightly beaten

A squeeze of lemon juice—about lemon's worth

½ cup whole, blanched almonds

2 tablespoons confectioners' sugar, plus extra for serving

1 lb. package phyllo dough leaves (available in the frozen-food section of the supermarket)

1. Put the chicken thighs, garlic, 2 tablespoons of parsley, shallot, saffron, ground ginger, ¼ teaspoon of the ground cinnamon, and 1 tablespoon of the butter in a medium-size saucepan along with ½ cup water, a pinch of salt, and a grinding of pepper. Bring the pot to a boil over medium heat, cover, and turn down the heat to low. Simmer the contents for 45 minutes, or until the chicken thighs are extremely tender and falling apart.

2. Remove the chicken from the pot, and set aside to cool. Meanwhile, turn up the heat and reduce the sauce by half, about 4 to 5 minutes. When you've done that, turn the heat back down to medium-low, and add the eggs, along with the squeeze of lemon juice, stirring the whole time. Cook the egg mixture until any excess moisture has boiled away—it should look like scrambled eggs when you're done, about 5 to 7 minutes more. Turn off the heat and transfer the eggs to a mixing bowl.

3. Shred the chicken thighs and add the meat to the mixing bowl, along with the remaining 2 tablespoons of parsley. Taste for salt. Mix to combine, then put in the fridge to cool.

NOT ON LOVE ALONE

4. In a small, dry frying pan over moderate heat, or in your toaster oven, toast the almonds until golden. Place them in the bowl of a food processor or blender along with the powdered sugar and remaining ¼ teaspoon cinnamon. Blend until it looks like fine crumbs. (Alternatively, you can chop the almonds fine with a chef's knife, then mix almonds, sugar, and cinnamon together in a bowl.)

5. Preheat the oven to 350°F.

6. Melt the remaining butter in the microwave and have it close at hand. Have the chicken mixture, a teaspoon, and the almond mixture standing by. Grease two baking sheets.

7. Prepare the phyllo. Phyllo is, to put it nicely, problematic. It'll make sailors of us all, language-wise. My best advice is, once you've taken it from the package and unrolled it, cover it immediately with a slightly damp kitchen towel and never let it see fresh air. Take out 2 sheets of phyllo from under its damp tent, and separate them. Brush one layer with butter, then place another sheet on top of that, and brush it with butter. Start at the corners and work your way to the middle—the phyllo stays put better that way. Cut the layered phyllo lengthwise into 3-inch-long strips.

8. Starting at one end of a strip of phyllo, place 1 teaspoon of chicken on the phyllo and top it with a hearty pinch (about ½ teaspoon) of the almonds. Place the filling at an angle so that you can fold the pastry over it and create the beginnings of a triangle. Keep folding the phyllo over itself, creating one triangle after another, like folding a flag. When you've folded the whole thing up, brush it with another bit of butter, then place it on the baking sheet.

9. Repeat steps 7 and 8 until all the phyllo and filling are used up.

10. Pop the *pastillas* in the oven and bake for 15 minutes, or until golden. These can be made ahead of time, and reheated in a low oven at party time.

11. To serve, sift a touch of confectioners' sugar over the top and cut the *pastillas* in half for easier eating.

SPECIAL EQUIPMENT: *A food processor is nice, but not necessary. A pastry brush, however, is necessary.*
TIME: *2 hours, some of it unattended*
FEEDS: *Makes 36 pastillas*

Gougères (Cheese Puffs)

I always make these. They are a snap—as long as you have all the ingredients on the counter, ready to go when you start—and though the recipe makes many, they're easily frozen and reheated in my favorite appliance, the toaster oven.

1 cup water or chicken stock (homemade or canned)

1 stick unsalted butter, cut into a few pieces

1 teaspoon kosher salt

1 cup flour

4 eggs, plus 1 for an egg wash

1½ cups grated Gruyère or Swiss cheese

Sea salt

1. Preheat the oven to 375°F. Line 2 rimmed baking sheets with parchment paper.
2. Put the stock, butter, and salt in a medium-size saucepan, and bring to a boil over high heat, stirring with a wooden spoon. As soon as all the butter is melted and the stock is rolling, turn off the heat and dump all the flour in the pot. Give the mixture a good wallop with a wooden spoon until all the lumps are gone and the mixture is smooth, like paste. Put the pot back over a low flame, stirring constantly, for about a minute (you want to dry out the dough slightly).
3. Transfer the hot dough to the bowl of a standing mixer or another mixing bowl. On medium speed, incorporate the 4 eggs, one after the other, beating in between each addition until the eggs are completely incorporated. The dough should be a smooth, sunny yellow, and still quite warm. Add the shredded cheese and mix to combine.
4. Fill a pastry bag or zip-top bag (see Pastry Bag Ins and Outs, page 212) with the *gougère* dough, and pipe out tablespoon-size amounts, about 1 inch apart, in long rows on the baking sheet.
5. When all the dough is piped out, mix the remaining egg with 1 teaspoon of water to make an egg wash. Then, using a small pastry brush or (my preference) a clean finger, daub the tops of the little mounds of dough with some egg wash. Follow that with a nice sprinkling of sea salt.
6. Bake the puffs for 10 minutes at 375° F, then lower the heat to 325°F and bake for 15 to 20 minutes more, or until the puffs are golden brown. Try to resist taking a peek for at least the first 15 minutes, or the *gougères* may not reach the majestic heights desired. Serve warm. (These are easily made ahead and frozen—just reheat them in a low oven for 5 minutes.)

SPECIAL EQUIPMENT: *If you're feeling very fancy, you need a standing mixer and a pastry bag fitted with a ½-inch tip. But the truth is, you can make these with a hand mixer, or even a wooden spoon, and a zip-top bag for the piping.*

TIME: *40 minutes*

FEEDS: *This recipe makes about 50 cheese puffs.*

ᴗ A NOTE ON BUTTER ᴗ

*J*USE ONLY UNSALTED butter, because it's what I grew up with. It's handy to cook with—and an absolute to bake with—because you can control how much salt there is going into your recipe.

For buttering bread, I like French butter, which has a higher milk-fat content than regular butter—and more milk fat means more flavor. That's just the way it is.

SALTED

SWEET
(THIS IS WHAT
I USE)

FANCY FRENCH BUTTER
-for-
SPECIAL OCCASIONS

Pastry Bag Ins and Outs

I̶T CAN TAKE a bit of time to get used to using a pastry bag. Here are some troubleshooting tips:

- You can make filling a pastry bag easier by resting it, tip down, in a drinking glass. That way both hands can concentrate on keeping the bag open and scooping in whatever you're piping.

- When the bag is full, give it a good jog or two to remove any air bubbles from within. This will prevent any embarrassing piping-bag explosions.

- Pipe with two hands. Twist the top of the bag closed with your dominant hand, and use it to keep constant pressure on the filling so it comes out at an even rate. The other hand can guide the tip.

- Practice a few times and expect a few mistakes.

Making a zip-top pastry bag: Just fill the bag with whatever you need to pipe, and seal it, forcing any excess air out of the bag. Cut off one corner to the aperture you need and pipe away. Best part? Easy cleanup.

FOR EASE
-of-
FILLING

USE BOTH HANDS

ZIP-TOP
BAG

WATER
GLASS

TEST SQUIRT

CUT HERE

Fried Veggies

Who doesn't like fried things? Certainly I like them, as this book has illustrated. These veggies can be made earlier in the day, kept at room temperature, and served au naturel or with a little dip, such as a light tomato sauce, a yogurt–dill sauce, or just a bit of crème fraîche with lemon juice and parsley.

I'm including two batters here, one with cheese and one without. I've suggested some vegetables that hold up well in batter, but feel free to experiment: look at the art on page 215 for suggestions.

FOR THE VEGETABLES:

2 bulbs fennel, washed and trimmed, cut into ¼-inch slices

½ head cauliflower, washed and trimmed into medium-size florets

1 sweet potato or butternut squash, peeled and shredded on a box grater

FOR THE SIMPLE BATTER:

⅓ cup all-purpose flour

¼ cup seltzer water

Pinch of kosher salt

FOR THE FANCY BATTER:

⅓ cup all-purpose flour

¼ cup seltzer water

Pinch of kosher salt

1 egg

⅓ cup finely grated Parmesan cheese

1 tablespoon finely chopped fresh flat-leaf parsley

Neutral oil (such as canola or safflower), for frying

Sea salt and lemon wedges, for serving

1. Get a steamer going on the stove. First steam the fennel for 3 minutes, then the cauliflower for 4 minutes. Let the vegetables cool on paper towels.
2. Prepare the simple batter: Sift the flour into a medium-size bowl, then slowly whisk in the seltzer. Add the salt. Then, in a separate bowl, prepare the fancy batter: Repeat the previous steps with the flour, seltzer, and salt, then add the egg and mix gently until completely combined. Fold in the cheese and parsley.
3. Heat a large skillet over a medium flame. Fill the skillet ¼ inch deep with vegetable oil and heat until shimmering. Test the heat by dropping a bit of bread into the oil. If it sizzles and browns within 20 seconds, it's ready to go. Prepare a cookie rack by placing it over paper towels.
4. Start with the fennel. Dip it in the simple batter, letting any excess drip back into the bowl, and lay it gently into the hot oil, leading away from your body to pre-

vent splatters. Continue adding the fennel without crowding the pan (you may need to cook it in batches), turning it once, until it's golden brown. Retrieve the fennel with tongs or a strainer, and then let cool on the cookie rack.

5. Next, the cauliflower. Using the fancy batter, dip and fry the cauliflower pieces as you did the fennel, regulating the heat under the skillet if things are getting too brown too quickly. Drain them the same way.

6. Finally, the sweet potato. Mix the shredded sweet potato with the remaining fancy batter. Transfer heaping tablespoonfuls to the hot oil, frying them until they're golden brown on each side. These will take a bit longer than the other vegetables, about 7 minutes a side, because you want to be sure that the potato cooks completely. Make sure the little patties aren't too thick—press them down if they're taller than they are wide. These should be drained on the cookie rack, too.

7. The nicest way to serve these is in mounds on parchment paper, with sea salt and lemon wedges on the side. If you can serve them hot, that's great, but I find them just as delicious warm or at room temperature.

SPECIAL EQUIPMENT: *A bamboo-handled strainer or tongs for flipping and removing the fried vegetables*
TIME: *A good bit of time for the prepping and frying in batches—at least 40 minutes*
FEEDS: *This recipe makes about 50 pieces.*

Winter Entertaining

❧

In the winter, particularly around the holidays, the food needs to be copious, the drinks generous, and the lighting flattering. While in the summer we all look good with our late-summer tans in the fading sunlight, by December, the best of us need some nicely dimmed lights and the flicker of dozens of votive candles. And, instead of festooning the entire place in Douglas fir, why not buy lots of tulips, which are everywhere in December, in one color, strip off their leaves, and lean them in great bunches in glass vases?

It's nicer to start cocktails a bit earlier than in the summer, since the sun disappears so early and, baby, it gets cold outside late.

In terms of food, I like a good variety (as is evident here) scattered about a room so people don't all congregate in one place. These recipes, plus a few cheeses, some long breadsticks, and maybe some charcuterie—cured ham and the like—would make for plenty of food for your guests on a long night of snacking and talking.

As for alcohol, I suggest (as I did in the summer) limiting the selection to one drink with the hard stuff, plus a selection of wine and beer. December nights lend themselves particularly well to bubbly things.

At a party with a larger spread, a bit of dessert is a welcome addition. The éclairs here are a real showstopper, but anything—cupcakes, brownies—will be hoovered up by the assembled hordes.

If you're thinking of having a New Year's party, even if it's at home, I would send out invitations (real letters! real stamps!) and suggest a dress code. We wear jeans the rest of the year—on one night we can look respectable.

Water Chestnuts Wrapped in Bacon

These couldn't be more old-fashioned. A fancier version of this recipe calls for wrapping the bacon around sea scallops, but I believe that's a waste of perfectly good sea scallops. The water chestnuts are easier and significantly cheaper, and the sweet crunch is lovely with the smoky bacon. It would be a good idea to assign the task of making these to whoever is less handy in the kitchen, since it's just manual labor.

1 (8-ounce) package thin-cut bacon	1 (8-ounce) can whole water chestnuts

1. Preheat the oven to 400°F.
2. Cut several strips of bacon into 3-inch lengths. Drain the water chestnuts and wrap each one in a length of bacon, securing the bacon with a toothpick. Put the water chestnuts on a rimmed baking sheet.
3. Slide the sheet into the oven and bake for 15 minutes, or until the bacon has rendered and is crispy. Pull from the oven, drain on paper towels, and serve hot.

SPECIAL EQUIPMENT: *Toothpicks!*
TIME: *20 minutes*
FEEDS: *This makes about 25 bacon-wrapped chestnuts.*

Fromage!

a Cheese Play in Five Acts

ACT FIVE: Party of Five

SCENE: *Saturday afternoon. J rushes into Murray's Cheese shop and makes a beeline for the counter. After she waits impatiently on line, CIELO finally has time for her.*

J, *desperately*. I need party cheese!

CIELO, *calm, collected*. For how many people, lady? Three hundred?

J. Almost! Twenty-five!

PETIT
BASQUE

PETIT
ROBERT

CIELO. What about a platter of five cheeses?

J, *nervous*. But which ones? Can you just pick them out?

CIELO. Of course. I'll give you a blue, Great Hill, from Massachusetts. And a nice creamy French Pierre Robert. And this Dutch Roomano, it's hard like Parmesan. A nice American goat, Humboldt Fog. And a sheep's-milk from the Pyrenees, Petit Basque. OK, lady? I'll just put you down for five hundred dollars' worth of cheese [wink].

J, *greatly relieved*. You're a lifesaver!

ROOMANO

GREAT
HILL
BLUE

(*fin*)

HUMBOLDT
FOG

For more on Murray's Cheese Shop, visit www.murrayscheese.com.

Crème Brûlée Éclairs

These éclairs are a great mix: there's the tenderness of the éclair shell, the sweet creaminess of the pastry cream, and the hard candy top. The flavors are the same as in crème brûlée, but no blowtorch is necessary. Though it does take some time to make them, once you get the hang of the piping there's nothing too difficult about the process. The best piece of advice I can give is that you have all your ingredients measured and at hand before you start—things go quickly and you don't want to find yourself having to run to the fridge in the middle of the recipe.

FOR THE PASTRY CREAM:

2 cups whole milk

½ vanilla bean, split lengthwise

6 egg yolks

⅔ cup sugar

¼ cup cornstarch

1 teaspoon cold unsalted butter

FOR THE ÉCLAIR SHELLS:

½ cup water

½ cup whole milk

1½ teaspoons sugar

½ teaspoon salt

1 stick butter, cubed

1 cup all-purpose flour

4 eggs

FOR THE TOP:

1¼ cup sugar

⅓ cup water

Prepare the pastry cream:

1. In a medium-size saucepan, heat the milk with the split vanilla bean until it comes to a boil. Keep an eye on it—this is not the time to learn how quickly milk can boil over and make a mess on your stove. As soon as it boils, cover the pan and turn off the heat, setting the milk aside for 10 minutes to steep.

2. In a large bowl, beat together the egg yolks and sugar with a mixer until they're lemon-colored and increased in bulk, about 3 minutes. Whisk in the cornstarch until no lumps remain.

3. Quickly incorporate ½ cup of the milk into the egg base (this, for the technical-minded among us, is called tempering and it prevents the shock of the hot milk from curdling the eggs, a bummer indeed). Once that ½ cup is incorporated, mix in the remaining milk in a steady stream, then pour everything *back* into the pot, through a sieve to catch the vanilla beans and any lumps of cornstarch. Stir

the whole shebang continually over medium heat until the mixture begins to thicken and comes to a lazy boil, probably no more than 2 minutes. Be diligent in your stirring. When it has thickened, turn off the heat and swirl in the pat of butter. Transfer the pastry cream to a bowl and cover with plastic wrap, pressing the wrap directly onto the surface of the cream to prevent a film from forming. When it's cool, place it in the fridge for several hours or overnight.

Make the éclair shells:
1. Preheat the oven to 375°F. Line two rimmed cookie sheets with parchment paper.
2. It is absolutely imperative to have everything ready here, because this dough goes fast. In a medium-size saucepan, heat the water, milk, sugar, salt, and butter over high heat, stirring with a wooden spoon until the liquid is boiling and the butter has melted. Turn off the heat and immediately dump in the entire cup of flour, mixing energetically with the wooden spoon until the contents of the pot look like a smooth paste. Turn the heat back on to low and stir the dough continuously for 1 minute, letting the mixture dry out a bit. Then, transfer it to the bowl of a standing mixer or another mixing bowl placed close to your hand mixer. One by one, incorporate the eggs, making sure to beat the dough thoroughly before adding the next. The final result should be a smooth, shiny, slightly marigold-colored dough.
3. Fill your piping bag, fitted with a ½-inch tip, with the batter, and start piping little logs—about 1 inch wide and 2½ inches long, placed about 2 inches apart from each other—onto the parchment-lined cookie sheets. This batch should make about thirty éclair shells.
4. When you're done piping, pop the éclair shells into the oven, resisting your urge to check them, for 10 minutes; then turn down the oven to 325°F and bake for another 15 to 20 minutes, until they're golden and puffy. Pull them out of the oven and let them cool on their trays.

Top and fill the éclairs:
1. Once everything is cool, fill your pastry bag with the pastry cream and set it aside in the refrigerator. Grease a cookie sheet and set it on the counter. Prepare a large ice bath by filling a mixing bowl or pan with ice cubes. Set it nearby on the counter as well.
2. Now, prepare the topping for the éclairs. Put the sugar in a small, heavy-bottomed saucepan (the sides should not be very high) and gently pour the water over it, running a finger through the sugar to make sure everything is moistened. Then don't touch it! Turn on the heat to medium-high and let the sugar water cook, gently swirling it once or twice until you have a nice amber caramel, about 10

minutes. Immediately take it off the heat and put the bottom of the pan in the ice bath for 30 seconds to stop the cooking. Take the pan out of the ice bath, move the ice bath away from your cooking surface, and start carefully dipping the éclair shells, tops down, into the (very, very hot) sugar and placing them, caramel side down, on the cookie sheet. I suggest using tongs to hold the éclair shells if you're nervous about getting your fingers close to hot sugar. If the caramel starts to harden, you can apply some more heat to the pot to loosen it up. The éclair tops will harden within minutes.

3. Finally, take the piping bag full of pastry cream, pick up a topped éclair, and, poking the tip in one end of the éclair, pipe a squirt of cream in the middle, without piping so much that it weighs a pound and explodes. Put the finished éclairs on a platter top side up and, once you've finished them all, cover and put them in the fridge until you're ready to eat.

⁓

SPECIAL EQUIPMENT: *A pastry bag with a metal tip (or a snipped zip-top bag—see Pastry Bag Ins and Outs, page 212); a hand-held or standing mixer; parchment paper for lining cookie sheets; an ice bath in a bowl large enough to hold the pot of hot sugar*
TIME: *About 1½ hours, including baking time*
FEEDS: *A recipe makes about 30 miniature éclairs.*

Éclair Variations

Уou don't need me to tell you that the world of éclairs is a large and varied one. Why don't you:

- Use the chocolate ganache recipe from February (page 40) to top the éclairs, instead of the caramel.
- Add 2 ounces of chopped, semisweet chocolate to the hot pastry cream to have . . . chocolate pastry cream. Or add a little instant espresso to that for mocha pastry cream.
- You can fill the éclairs with orange or lemon curd, too.
- Why not make a quick icing (water, confectioners' sugar, almond extract) and dip the tops in that, then in toasted, slivered almonds.
- Or, in the springtime, crush some strawberries in confectioners' sugar with a drop of water, and have strawberry éclairs.

You can tell I'm a serious éclair scholar.

WINTER TIPPLES

I think I've mentioned before that I don't drink hard alcohol very often, and when I forget myself and do, I am always very, very sorry. But that doesn't mean our friends shouldn't wake up the day after a party with pounding headaches and blurry vision!

Also included here is a list of single-malt Scotches recommended by my friend Weatherly Ralph, whom I've quoted in part, à la *Zagat*, on page 226.

imm's is a terrific summertime drink, a sort of British sangria, but I think this version, with the extra kick of vodka and the concentration on oranges and lemons, makes it a great wintertime drink, too.

2 cups Pimm's

2 cups San Pellegrino Limonata (a tart, fizzy drink)

½ cup any decent vodka

1 orange, sectioned (see page 101)

1 grapefruit, sectioned (see page 101)

1 lemon, thinly sliced

½ Granny Smith apple, cored and cut into thin crescents

Gently stir together all of the ingredients in a large pitcher, and serve in tumblers over lots of ice.

QUENCHES: *The thirst of 6*

NOT ON LOVE ALONE

The Stinking Bishop

A hot drink with a spectacular presentation. I don't know where the name comes from, as the stinking bishop is also a (indeed very stinky) cheese. I assume this drink has English origins, and suggests that your average British bishop is not only lacking in personal hygiene, but drunk as a lord as well.

2 lemons	½ cup Cognac
1 cup superfine sugar	2¼ cups boiling water
1 cup dark rum	

1. Zest and juice the lemons and set the juice aside. In a large flameproof bowl (or punch bowl) mix together the zest, sugar, and dark rum.
2. Put the Cognac in a flameproof measuring cup or pan. Heat the Cognac for 30 seconds in the microwave, or on top of the stove for a minute. If you've heated it on a stove, remove it from the heat and any flame. Then, carefully, flambé it with a match and pour it into the bowl. Add the boiling water and reserved lemon juice, and serve hot in little punch cups.

QUENCHES: *12 revelers*

Weatherly's Single-Malt List

J COULDN'T TELL a single-malt Scotch from bathtub gin, so I turned to my friend Weatherly Ralph for advice. She has spent enough time in the UK, throwing down shots with lords and locals alike, to know what she is talking about.

In fact, the only time I've gotten close to single-malt Scotch was with Weath, while she was a graduate student at Oxford. I happened to eat dinner with her in the hall at Christ Church College on Robbie Burns night, which involves some poetry reading, some haggis with neeps and tatties (recipes decidedly not included here), and lots of single-malt to wash it all down with. The last thing I remember is dancing to Duran Duran's "The Reflex"—a lower form of poetic expression than Burns's "To a Mouse," perhaps, but just as compelling in its way.

Here are a few Weatherly reviews of single-malt Scotches:

Laphroaig 10-Year-Old Scotch: "Very salty and peaty," this lively Scotch from the island of Islay in Scotland is a bona fide "man drink," meant to be sipped slowly on the coldest nights of the year. Best neat or with a little water.

Edradour Single Malt: From Great Britain's smallest distillery "in the Highlands" comes this "lighter" "delicious" Scotch, with berry notes and a rich, gold hue. Best of all? "Ladies can drink it."

Cragganmore Single Malt (12 Year): "A good all-around Scotch" for single-malt neophytes, this "fragrant" Scotch has some sweet notes to offset the anticipated burn.

Macallan (12 Year): Aged in sherry oak, it's a robust, spicy Scotch. It's no wonder that "older men love this one."

The Weekender

This was a drink invented by our friend Joe Piech on vacation . . . when you have all day to invent things like this. And drink things like this.

2 cups freshly squeezed orange juice

1 cup club soda

1 cup gin, of a decent variety

Orange slices, to float on the top

In a large pitcher, gently stir together the orange juice, club soda, and gin. Pour over ice and add a slim slice of orange to each drink.

QUENCHES: *6 drinkers*

Real Tom Collins

This version comes from a friend who has a masters in mixology from a course he took at Yale University. Well, I don't know if it was an accredited course, but I like to think so.

¼ cup good gin

2 tablespoons freshly squeezed lemon juice

1 teaspoon superfine sugar

⅓ cup club soda

Add the gin, lemon juice, and sugar to a cocktail shaker with some ice and shake, baby. Strain it into a cocktail glass filled with ice and add the club soda.

QUENCHES: *Just 1. Multiply ad infinitum.*

ANNIVERSARY

And Many More

And Many More

STILL CLAIMS that the first multicourse, complicated meal I cooked him—for an early "anniversary" of ours—is the best thing I've ever made. Though sometimes exasperated by this sentiment—I think of the hundreds of my meals he's eaten between then and now—I'm always touched by his dogged insistence. It's the romance of the thing.

That meal was entirely made out of Julia Child's *Mastering the Art of French Cooking,* and included such fussy standbys as lobster with mayonnaise and beef tenderloin with cèpes. In honor of it, I've made the main course here lobster, though with slightly less mayo and grated tomalley involved.

The meal should be easy, and not dreadfully heavy, though it depends on how overboard you go on the foie gras. After all, the point of an anniversary dinner is to admire each other and impress yourselves with how lucky you are.

And though I seem to pop the cork in a bottle of Champagne at the least provocation, if there's any time to drink some, it's now.

*Here's to a year . . .
and many more*

FOIE GRAS WITH BRIOCHE (PAGE 232)

&

LOBSTER GRATINÉED WITH HERB BUTTER (PAGE 234)

&

BRAISED BOSTON LETTUCE HEARTS (PAGE 236)

&

CHOCOLATE POTS DE CRÈME (PAGE 237)

Foie Gras with Brioche

There's absolutely no cooking involved here, only assembling.

Foie gras: Of goose, please, not duck. Either a mousse of foie gras, which is a less-expensive pâté, or (what's much better) the pricier terrine of foie gras, where the whole lobes are cooked together. This is beyond delicious, and it's so rich you can get a very small amount. The best source for this is D'Artagnan, a company based in New Jersey, and the smallest portion they sell of the terrine is half a pound, which is, in the words of my mother, a plentiful sufficiency for two people (www.dartagnan.com).

Brioche: The best bakery around will have little individual brioches, or a small loaf, which you should slice into sandwich-bread thickness and toast well. In a pinch, you could use a good-quality challah (though the idea makes me weep).

Unsalted butter: Because there's not enough fat in the foie gras as it is. Buy the fanciest French butter from Normandy you can find.

Sea salt: Need I say this should be the sort of salt that has a better pedigree than most of the dogs at the Westminster Dog Show?

Presentation: Just slice a good slab of chilled terrine of foie gras and lay it on a plate, served with a few curls of butter and a small pile of sea salt. Serve the toasted brioche on a small plate on the side.

TIME: *Mere moments*
FEEDS: *2 lucky souls*

Foie Gras Go-Withs

𝒯RADITIONALLY, FOIE GRAS is paired with Sauternes, a concentrated sweet wine, or other sweet wines. You can get versions of these sweet white wines across the price spectrum and from California, France, and Italy. The best part is that they're widely available in half bottles, perfect for two.

Pops, who knows his wine, recommends the modestly priced Vin de Glacière by California producer Bonny Doon.

Sides for Foie Gras

If you want to gild the lily, you could serve dainty portions of the following:

- Fig preserves
- Red currant jelly
- Toasted, chopped hazelnuts
- Thin slices of Anjou pear
- A few sliced prunes
- Shaved black truffle
- A small pool of very high-quality balsamic vinegar

Lobster Gratinéed *with* Herb Butter

How much work you do on this dish is a question of how much control you want over the lobster. At fancier markets and fish stores, you can get lobsters presteamed, which keeps you from having to send the big fellas to their death yourself. It does, however, keep you from being in control of how cooked (or, sadly, overcooked) the lobster is. The final decision is up to you.

FOR THE LOBSTERS:

2 live lobsters—make sure they're very lively—each about 1½ pounds

Kosher salt

FOR THE COMPOUND BUTTER:

4 tablespoons unsalted butter, very soft

1 tablespoon finely chopped fresh flat-leaf parsley

1 teaspoon finely snipped fresh chives

½ teaspoon finely chopped fresh tarragon

1 teaspoon lemon zest

½ teaspoon kosher salt

Chopped fresh flat-leaf parsley, for garnish

1. If you're taking care of the lobster business yourself, put the critters in a bowl and place them in your freezer for at least 30 minutes to induce a lobstery coma.

2. Meanwhile, bring a large pot of salted water to a boil over high heat. Make sure the pot has a lid that fits. When the water is really rolling, slide the chilly lobsters into the water, where they will immediately start turning red. When the water comes back to a boil, cook the lobsters for 12 minutes. Pull them from the water and let cool. You can do this earlier in the day and refrigerate the cooked lobsters until you need them.

3. While the lobsters are cooling off, make the compound butter. Mix all the ingredients in a small bowl with a rubber spatula, then scrape the whole mess onto a piece of waxed paper. Roll up the butter in the paper and shape into a log. Pop it into the freezer to let it set up, for at least 15 minutes (you can make it ahead and keep it there, but move it to the fridge to soften before using it).

4. Preheat the broiler.

5. Cut the lobsters in half along the axis of their bodies, so each half has a claw and the cross-section of a tail. Pull out the not-so-nice contents of the head and chest cavity, and scrape out the green tomalley. Crack the claws and pull out the meat, placing it in the now cleaned chest cavity, along with any meat you get out of the joints. Arrange it so it looks pretty, but make sure it's not sticking up too

far, or you might have an unhappy result in the broiler. You can prepare this several hours in advance and keep, covered, in the fridge. Take them out of the cold for half an hour to take the chill off before you pop them into the broiler.

6. Place each half (4 total) cut side up on a broiling pan or rimmed baking sheet. Top each half with a quarter of the herb butter, making sure to get a bit on the claw meat. Slide the pan into the broiler and broil until the butter is melted and there's some nice golden color on the tail, about 3 to 5 minutes.

7. Pull the lobsters from the broiler and arrange them prettily on a plate, dusting them with parsley. Serve them with Braised Boston Lettuce Hearts (recipe follows).

TIME: *Just a few minutes to prepare the butter and broil the lobster, another 20 minutes if you plan on cooking the lobster yourself*
FEEDS: *2 in a celebratory mood*

Braised Boston Lettuce Hearts

Sometimes you can find very small heads of Boston lettuce, which are perfect for this. If not, buy a larger head and take off some of the outer leaves so you get to the pale green heart. Braising is an overstatement here; it's more of a somersault in lemon and cream in a pan before joining the lobster on the plate.

4 tiny, or 2 small heads Boston lettuce, washed and dried, a few outer leaves removed, but kept intact—trim and discard any browned parts at the base (the end result should be 2 hearts, each about the size of a softball)

1 teaspoon butter

3 tablespoons heavy cream

1 tablespoon fresh lemon juice

1 teaspoon lemon zest

Sea salt and freshly ground black pepper

Cut the lettuce hearts in half lengthwise. Heat a medium-size skillet over high heat. Melt the butter, let the foaming subside, and then add the cream, lemon juice, lemon zest, and some salt and grindings of pepper. Add the lettuce hearts and swirl them about the pan, flipping them over with tongs until the outer leaves just start to wilt, about 30 seconds. Serve with the lobster.

TIME: *Just a minute or two in a hot pan*
FEEDS: *2 lovebirds*

NOT ON LOVE ALONE

Chocolate Pots de Crème

These rich custards will make you happy without weighing you down.

2 cups half-and-half	6 egg yolks
½ vanilla bean, split	⅓ cup sugar
2 ounces high-quality semisweet chocolate, such as Lindt, chopped	¼ cup sifted Dutch-process cocoa powder

1. Preheat the oven to 325°F.
2. Bring the half-and-half to a simmer in a small saucepan with the vanilla bean; cover the pan and turn off the heat. Wait for 5 minutes, then rescue the vanilla pod from the pot. Turn on the heat to low and add the chopped semisweet chocolate, whisking until the chocolate is completely melted. Turn off the heat, cover, and set aside for a moment.
3. In a medium-size mixing bowl, whisk the egg yolks with the sugar until lemon-colored and light; then whisk in the cocoa powder until just combined, without lumps. Whisking continually and furiously, add ½ cup of the hot chocolate half-and-half to the eggs to temper them. Then, add the remaining chocolate half-and-half to the egg mixture. Strain the custard through a sieve into another mixing bowl, making sure no bits of egg yolk get into the bowl.
4. Ladle the chocolate custard into the ramekins or pots, dividing it evenly among them. If using ramekins, cover the tops with a bit of tinfoil to prevent a skin from forming during baking. Put a roasting pan in the oven and place the ramekins in it. Carefully pour boiling water into the pan until there's ½ inch around the ramekins.
5. Bake these little custards for 25 minutes, or until they are mostly set but still a little wobbly in the middle. Overbaking makes them too dense—the chocolate flavor is intense, but the texture should be soft and light. They're perfect on their own, chilled from the refrigerator.

SPECIAL EQUIPMENT: *You need six 4-ounce ramekins or pots de crème*
TIME: *Less than an hour of work, plus time to let the pots cool in the fridge*
FEEDS: *This makes 6—a couple for the anniversary night and some for later.*

First-Anniversary Gifts

THE THEME IS paper, liberally interpreted:

- 🙠 An early edition of a favorite book
- 🙠 Personalized stationery
- 🙠 Tickets to a play or a show
- 🙠 A map of an upcoming vacation destination
- 🙠 A print of a favorite painting or other work of art

Index

African Marinade, 102

alcohol, serving, 152, 217. *See also* beverages; cocktail parties

allspice, ideas for, 110

almonds, toasting, 144

Anniversary, 229–238

Apples, Sautéed, with Vanilla, 185

Applesauce, 26

Applesauce Cake, 76

Apricot-Thyme Clafouti, 130

April, 61–79

arborio rice, 8

Artichoke Hearts and Peas, Herb-Braised, 64

artichokes, 62, 66–67

Asian Marinade, 102

asparagus, 71
  and mint risotto, 161
  roasted, 65

August, 133–154

Bacon, Water Chestnuts Wrapped in, 218

bain-marie water bath, 195

basil, 156, 163
  Farfalle with Ricotta, Lemon, Basil, and Peas, 165
  Fusilli with Zucchini, Garlic, and Basil, 164
  Spaghetti Pesto with Croutons, 166

basmati rice, 8

beans, dried, 200. *See also* green beans
  as pie weights, 55
  in Soupe au Pistou, 116–118
  Spicy Chickpeas, 207

beef, 20, 121
  Rib of Beef on the Grill, 121
  Veal, Braised, with Mushroom Ragout and Garlic Toasts, 18

beets, steaming, 180

Belgian mussel pot, 58

Bellinis, 151

bento boxes, 188, 192
  Edamame, 192
  Fennel and Radish Salad, 193
  Frittata Wrap, 190

beverages
  Bellinis, 151
  Cava, 43

Champagne, 42–43
  orange juice and gin, 227
  Pimm's, Fortified, 224
  Pineapple Vodka Tonics, 154
  Prosecco, 43
  Single-Malt Scotch (list), 226
  The Stinking Bishop, 225
  Tom Collins, 227
  wine, 60, 152

Blueberries, Relaxed, and Vanilla Ice Cream, 114

Boston Lettuce Hearts, Braised, 236

bouquet garni, 23

breakfasts
  Applesauce Cake, 76
  Cinnamon Sticky Buns, 78
  Peach Tart, Fast, 162
  Scottish Cream Scones, 77

brioche, 232

broccoli rabe, 181

Brussels sprouts, 180, 200

butter, 9, 211

Butternut Squash, Orecchiette with Lentils, Cream, and, 182

butternut squash risotto, 161

cabbage, 200

Caprese salad, 128–129

Caprese salad on bread, 94

caraway seeds, ideas for, 110

cardamom pods, ideas for, 110

Carrot Soufflé, 195

cauliflower, 181

Cauliflower Soup with Cumin Seeds and Parsley, 198

Cava, 43

Champagne, 42–43

Cheese!, 38, 89, 124, 168, 219

Cheese Puffs, 210

chestnuts, 199, 201, 218

chicken, 139. *See also* meats
  Chicken, Roasted, with Watercress, 138
  Chicken Noodle Soup, 22–25
  Chicken Soup with Ginger, Barley, and Chestnuts, 199
  Fried Chicken, Sort of, 84
  Moroccan Pastillas, Mini, 208

Chickpeas, Spicy, 207
chocolate ganache, 40
Chocolate Pots de Crème, 237
Chocolate Sauce for Ice Cream, 125
cinnamon, oranges sprinkled with, 39
Cinnamon Sticky Buns, 78
citrus fruit(s), 8, 101
    Citrus Desserts, Simple, 39
    citrus salad with sugar and Grand Marnier, 39
    grapefruit, sautéed, with fresh mint and mas-
        carpone, 39
    grapefruit with brown sugar, 39
    Lemon Ginger Cookies, 108
    Lemon Ginger Tart, 54
    lemons, preserving, 107
    orange sections with caramel sauce, 39
    oranges sprinkled with cinnamon, 39
Clafouti, Apricot-Thyme, 130
cocktail parties, 134, 145, 204–205, 216–217.
    See also beverages; hors d'oeuvres
comfort foods, 14, 22
cookies
    Lace Cookies, 21
    Lemon Ginger Cookies, 108
    Pinwheel Cookies, 90
corn, cutting from the cob, 142
Corn Griddle Cakes, 141
couscous, cooking, 107
Couscous and Other Good Food from Morocco
    (Wolfert), 107
Couscous Salad with Carrots, Pine Nuts, and
    Orange, 100
Crème Brûlé Éclairs, 220–223
Les Crêpes Célèbre de Mère Blanc, 176
Cucumber Salad, 88
cumin, ideas for, 110

December, 203–227
desserts. *See also* cookies
    about pastries, 53
    Apples, Sautéed, with Vanilla, 185
    Apricot-Thyme Clafouti, 130
    Blueberries, Relaxed, and Vanilla Ice Cream, 114
    Chocolate Pots de Crème, 237
    Chocolate Sauce for Ice Cream, 125
    Citrus Desserts, Simple, 39
    citrus salad with sugar and Grand Marnier, 39
    Crème Brûlé Éclairs, 220–223
    Les Crêpes Célèbre de Mère Blanc, 176
    Doughnut Bites with Chocolate Ganache

Filling, 40
    grapefruit, sautéed, with fresh mint and mas-
        carpone, 39
    grapefruit with brown sugar, 39
    Ice Cream with Caramel and Toasted
        Almonds, 144
    Lace Cookies, 21
    Lemon Ginger Cookies, 108
    Lemon Ginger Tart, 54
    orange sections with caramel sauce, 39
    oranges sprinkled with cinnamon, 39
    Peach Tart, Fast, 162
    Pears, Baked, with Brown Sugar, 178
    Pinwheel Cookies, 90
    strawberry torte, 72
    Torte, Wrong Way, 72
dinner parties, 12, 134, 152–153, 184, 194
dinners. *See* main course
Doughnut Bites with Chocolate Ganache Filling,
    40
drinks. *See* beverages

Éclair Variations, 223
Éclairs, Crème Brûlé, 220–223
Edamame, 192
eggs, 74
    Carrot Soufflé, 195
    Egg Drop Soup with Mint, 197
    Hollandaise Sauce, 180
    Quail Eggs with Celery Salt, 145
Essentials of Classic Italian Cooking (Hazan), 106

Fall Vegetables with Hollandaise Sauce, 180
Farfalle with Ricotta, Lemon, Basil, and Peas, 165
farmers' market, 62, 143
Faux Greek Marinade, 103
February, 27–43
fennel
    bulbs, steaming, 180
    Fennel and Radish Salad, 193
    Fennel and Tapenade on Toast, 148
first course. *See* side dishes
First-Anniversary Gifts, 238
fish, 46. *See also* seafood
    Fish Fillets Meunière, 52
    Niçoise salad on a bun, 93
    in Pan Bagna, Mini, 93
    Salade Niçoise Composée, 126
    in Salade Niçoise Composée, 126
    salmon, smoked, in frittata wrap, 190

Watercress Salad with Smoked Trout, 16
foie gras, 232
Fois Gras Go-Withs, 233
Fois Gras with Brioche, 232
food mills, 6
France, 116
French Potato Salad, 87
Fried Chicken, Sort of, 84
Frittata Wrap, 190
Fromage!, 38, 89, 124, 168, 219
fruits. *See also* citrus fruits
fruit(s)
    Apples, Sautéed, with Vanilla, 185
    Applesauce, 26
    Applesauce Cake, 76
    Apricot-Thyme Clafouti, 130
    baking, 178
    Bellinis (peaches), 151
    herbs and, 131
    Peach Tart, Fast, 162
    Pears, Baked, with Brown Sugar, 178
    Pineapple Vodka Tonics, 154
    strawberry torte, 72
Fusilli with Zucchini, Garlic, and Basil, 164

game, shopping for, 174
garlic, 9, 137
garlic toasts, 18
ginger, 9
    Chicken Soup with Ginger, Barley, and
      Chestnuts, 199
    Lemon Ginger Cookies, 108
    Lemon Ginger Tart, 54
Goat Cheese, Stuffed Zucchini with, 158
Gougères (Cheese Puffs), 210
Grand Marnier, 39
grapefruit. *See* citrus fruits
Greek Marinade, 103
Greek Yogurt, 9
green beans
    Green Bean and Hazelnut Salad, 48
    in salads, 46, 96
    in Soupe au Pistou, 116–118
green market, 62, 143
greens, 36–37, 138, 201. *See also* salads
Grilled Cheese (sandwich), 113
grilling beef, 121

ham and Gruyére sandwich, 95
Hazan, Marcella, 106

Hazelnut and Green Bean Salad, 48
hazelnut oil, 10
Herb-Braised Artichoke Hearts and Peas, 64
Herbes de Provence, 11
herbs, 96
Hollandaise Sauce, Fall Vegetables with, 180
hors d'oeuvres
    Chickpeas, Spicy, 207
    Fennel and Tapenade on Toast, 148
    Fois Gras with Brioche, 232
    Gougères (Cheese Puffs), 210
    Moroccan Pastillas, Mini, 208
    Quail Eggs with Celery Salt, 145
    Radishes with Butter and Salt, 149
    Rubbed Toast, 146
    Spiced Pecans, 206
    Squash Blossoms, Fried, 147
    Tomatoes stuffed with Feta and Chives, 150
    Veggies, Fried, 214
    Water Chestnuts Wrapped in Bacon, 218

ice cream. *See* desserts
Imitation Olive's Sandwich, 94

January, 13–26
July, 115–131
June, 97–114

kitchens, 5–7
knives, 6, 51, 66
kosher salt, 10, 140

Lace Cookies, 21
lactose-intolerance, 184
lamb, shopping for, 106
Lamb Tagine with Lemon and Olives, 104
lemon, parsley, and pine nut risotto, 161
lemons. *See* citrus fruits
lentils, 200
Lentils, Orecchiette with Butternut Squash,
    Cream, and, 182
lettuces, 36–37, 96, 128–129. *See also* salads
    Boston Lettuce Hearts, Braised, 236
Lobster Gratinéed with Herb Butter, 234
lunch. *See* sandwiches; soups and stews

mace, ideas for, 110
main course. *See also* pasta; soups and stews
    Fish Fillets Meunière, 52
    Lamb Tagine with Lemon and Olives, 104

Lobster Gratinéed with Herb Butter, 234
Pork Loin Braised in Milk, 68
Potatoes, Roasted, with Shallots and Toasted
    Walnuts, 35
Potatoes Aligote, 32
Potatoes Crique, 34
Rib of Beef on the Grill, 121
Roasted Chicken with Watercress, 138
Scallops, Seared, 59
Shrimp, Poached, 57
Veal, Braised, with Mushroom Ragout and
    Garlic Toasts, 18
mandolines, 6
March, 45–60
mascarpone, grapefruit, sautéed, with fresh mint
    and, 39
May, 81–95
mayonnaise, adding to, 95
meat thermometers, 6, 138
meats. *See also* chicken
meat(s)
    ham and Gruyére sandwich, 95
    Lamb Tagine with Lemon and Olives, 104
    Pork Loin Braised in Milk, 68
    prosciutto, on rubbed toast, 146
    Rabbit and Tomato Stew, 172
    Rib of Beef on the Grill, 121
    Veal, Braised, with Mushroom Ragout and
        Garlic Toasts, 18
    Water Chestnuts Wrapped in Bacon, 218
Mirepoix, 175
Moroccan Pastillas, Mini, 208
Morocco, 98, 107
mozzarella and tomato sandwich, 94
mushroom ragout, 18
mushroom risotto, 161
mushrooms, dried, 200
Mussels, Steamed, 58

Niçoise salad, 126
Niçoise salad on a bun, 93
North African Marinade, 102
November, 187–201
nuts, 8
    combining with vegetables, 49
    Couscous Salad with Carrots, Pine Nuts, and
        Orange, 100
    Green Bean and Hazelnut Salad, 48
    in Lace Cookies, 21
    Spiced Pecans, 206

October, 169–185
olive oil, 10
onions, 9
onions, pearl, 181
oranges. *See* citrus fruits
Orecchiette with Lentils, Butternut Squash, and
    Cream, 182

Pan Bagna, Mini, 93
Pan-Asian Marinade, 102
pantry, stocking the, 8–11, 73, 96, 200–201
paprika, ideas for, 110
parties. See also beverages; hors d'oeuvres; picnics
    cocktail, 134, 145, 204–205, 216–217
    dinner, 12, 134, 152–153, 184, 194
pasta, 8, 163
    Farfalle with Ricotta, Lemon, Basil, and Peas,
        165
    Fusilli with Zucchini, Garlic, and Basil, 164
    Orecchiette with Lentils, Butternut Squash,
        and Cream, 182
    Spaghetti Pesto with Croutons, 166
Pastillas, Mini Moroccan, 208
pastry bags, 212–213
pastry cream, 220
pastry primer, 53
peaches
    in Bellinis, 151
    Peach Tart, Fast, 162
pearl onions, 181
Pears, Baked, with Brown Sugar, 178
Pecans, Spiced, 206
pepper grinders, 6
peppercorns, 10
phyllo dough, 208, 209
picnics, 82, 86, 92
    Cucumber Salad, 88
    Edamame, 192
    Fennel and Radish Salad, 193
    French Potato Salad, 87
    Fried Chicken, Sort of, 84
    Frittata Wrap, 190
    picnic salads, 88
Pimm's, Fortified, 224
Pineapple Vodka Tonics, 154
Pinwheel Cookies, 90
pork, 70
    ham and Gruyére sandwich, 95
    Pork Loin Braised in Milk, 68
    prosciutto, on rubbed toast, 146

Not on Love Alone

Water Chestnuts Wrapped in Bacon, 218
potato ricers, 33, 177
potatoes, 30–31, 181
    Les Crêpes Célèbre de Mère Blanc, 176
    French Potato Salad, 87
    Potatoes, Roasted, with Shallots and Toasted
      Walnuts, 35
    Potatoes Aligote, 32
    Potatoes Crique, 34
pots and pans, 7, 58, 59, 69
pressure cookers, 24–25, 118–119
prosciutto, on rubbed toast, 146
Prosecco, 43
purple potatoes, 181

Quail Eggs with Celery Salt, 145

rabbit, 170, 174
Rabbit and Tomato Stew, 172
Radish and Fennel Salad, 193
Radishes with Butter and Salt, 149
ragout, mushroom, 18
Rib of Beef on the Grill, 121
Rice Pancakes, 112
Risotto, Tomato, 160
risotto madness, 161
root vegetables, ideas for, 201
Rubbed Toast, 146

saffron
    in Lamb Tagine with Lemon and Olives, 104
    in Moroccan Pastillas, 208
    in Mussels, Steamed, 58
salad dressings, 36–37, 128
salad(s)
    Caprese salad and variations, 128–129
    citrus salad with sugar and Grand Marnier, 39
    Couscous Salad with Carrots, Pine Nuts, and
      Orange, 100
    Cucumber Salad, 88
    Fennel and Radish Salad, 193
    French Potato Salad, 87
    for picnics, 88
    Salade Niçoise Composée, 126
    Summer Salad, 128–129
    Watercress Salad with Smoked Trout, 16
    Winter Salads, 36–37
salmon, smoked, in frittata wrap, 190
salt, 140
sandwiches

Frittata Wrap, 190
Grilled Cheese, 113
ham and Gruyére, 95
Imitation Olive's Sandwich, 94
mozzarella and tomato, 94
Pan Bagna, Mini, 93
Le Sandwich Mixte, 95
scallions, 181
Scallops, Seared, 59
Scones, Scottish Cream, 77
Scotch, Single-Malt, 226
Scottish Cream Scones, 77
sea salt, 9, 140
seafood, 56. See also fish
    Lobster Gratinéed with Herb Butter, 234
    Mussels, Steamed, 58
    Scallops, Seared, 59
    Shrimp, Poached, 57
September, 155–168
shallots, 9
shears, 6
Sherry vinegar, 10
shopping tips
    beef and veal for braising, 20
    eggs, 74
    farmers' market, 62, 143
    fish, 50–51
    Fromage!, 38, 89, 124, 168, 219
    garlic, 9
    green market, 62, 143
    healthy snacks, 191
    lamb cuts, 106
    pasta, 163
    pork, 70
    potatoes, 30–31
    rabbit and game, 174
Shrimp, Poached, 57
side dishes. See also salads
    Artichoke Hearts and Peas, Herb-Braised, 64
    Asparagus, Roasted, 65
    Carrot Soufflé, 195
    Corn Griddle Cakes, 141
    Les Crêpes Célèbre de Mère Blanc, 176
    Potatoes, Roasted, with Shallots and Toasted
      Walnuts, 35
    Potatoes Aligote, 32
    Potatoes Crique, 34
    Tomato Bruschetta, 136
    Tomatoes Provençal, 123
    Zucchini, Fried, 122

Single-Malt Scotch, 226
snacks, 111, 191. See also hors d'oeuvres
    Blueberries, Relaxed, and Vanilla Ice Cream, 114
    Grilled Cheese sandwiches, 113
    Rice Pancakes, 112
soups and stews
    Cauliflower Soup with Cumin Seeds and Parsley, 198
    Chicken Noodle Soup, 22–25
    Chicken Soup with Ginger, Barley, and Chestnuts, 199
    Egg Drop Soup with Mint, 197
    Rabbit and Tomato Stew, 172
    Soupe au Pistou, 116–118
Spaghetti Pesto with Croutons, 166
spatulas, 6
Spiced Pecans, 206
spices, 110, 140
Spicy Chickpeas, 207
Squash Blossoms, Fried, 147
The Stinking Bishop (drink), 225
strainers, 6
strawberry torte, 72
Summer Salad, 128–129

Tapenade and Fennel on Toast, 148
Thanksgiving detox, 196
    Cauliflower Soup with Cumin Seeds and Parsley, 198
    Chicken Soup with Ginger, Barley, and Chestnuts, 199
    Egg Drop Soup with Mint, 197
thyme, fresh, 11
toast, rubbed, 146
Tom Collins, 227
tomatoes, 96, 156
    canned, 10
    mozzarella and tomato sandwich, 94
    Rabbit and Tomato Stew, 172
    Tomato Bruschetta, 136
    Tomato Risotto, 160
    Tomatoes Provençal, 123

Tomatoes stuffed with Feta and Chives, 150
tongs, 6
Torte, Wrong Way, 72
Trout, Smoked, Watercress Salad with, 16
tumeric, ideas for, 110
tuna fish
    Niçoise salad on a bun, 93
    Pan Bagna, Mini, 93
    Salade Niçoise Composée, 126

utensils, 6–7, 33, 51, 53, 177

vanilla beans
    Apples, Sautéed, with Vanilla, 185
    in Apricot-thyme Clafouti, 130
    in Chocolate Pots de Crème, 237
    in Crème Brûlé Éclairs, 220–223
Veal, Braised, with Mushroom Ragout and Garlic Toasts, 18
vegetable peelers, 6
vegetables. See also specific vegetables
vegetable(s)
    Artichoke Hearts and Peas, Herb-Braised, 64
    combining with nuts, 49
    Fall Vegetables with Hollandaise Sauce, 180
vegetarian and vegans, 179
Veggies, Fried, 214
Vodka Tonics, Pineapple, 154

Water Chestnuts Wrapped in Bacon, 218
Watercress Salad with Smoked Trout, 16
wine, 60, 152
Winter Salads, 36–37
Wolfert, Paula, 107

Yogurt, Greek, 9
Yukon Gold potatoes, 31, 32
    in Soupe au Pistou, 116–118

zucchini, 156
    fried, 122
    Fusilli with Zucchini, Garlic, and Basil, 164
    Stuffed Zucchini with Goat Cheese, 158

NOT ON LOVE ALONE